From the Barstool To the Pulpit

*Looking For Love and
Not Knowing Where To Find It*

REBECCA J. WHITE

From the Barstool to the Pulpit
Copyright © 2008 Rebecca J. White
Leading Lady Publications
A Division of Anointed Word Media Group
Worton, MD 21678
www.publishyourchristianbook.com

ISBN-13: 978-0-9818753-3-0
ISBN-10: 0-9818753-3-5

Front Cover Graphic Design: Shamsud Din Katib Bey
Book Cover Design: Tamika Johnson-Hall
Copyedited by: Roz A. Gee (www.rozgee.com)

ALL RIGHTS RESERVED. No part of this publication may be reproduced in any manner whatsoever without written permission, except in case of brief quotations.

Printed in the United States of America

To order additional copies, please contact:
Anointed Word Media Group
1-800-597-9428
info@publishyourchristianbook.com
www.anointedwordbookstore.net

All scripture references are taken from the King James Version of the Bible.

BAR MENU	PRICE LIST
ACKNOWLEDGMENTS	5
INTRODUCTION	9
GROWING UP AND RAISING THE BAR!	13
SHATTERED GLASSES AND BROKEN DREAMS	19
SIN ON THE ROCKS	24
STIRRING UP LOVE	34
CHEERS, FEARS AND TEARS	41
REMOVIN' THE BLACK LABEL	47
BLOODY MARY OR BLOODY BECKY	51
SERVING UP THE USUAL	57
TONIC, TOXIC AND TOILET DRAMA	63
ON THE HOT SEAT OF DEFEAT	73
BAR ROOM BRAWLIN'	78
HERE'S ONE FOR THE ROAD!	86
STAGGERING BUT STILL STANDING	92
ANOTHER GOOD TIMES RERUN	98
LOOKING FOR LOVE	106

A TASTE OF GENESIS	114
BARSTOOL TRANSFORMATION	130
SHAKEN, NOT STIRRED	140
OLD WINE, NEW WINESKINS	152
TAB—PICKED UP AND PAID IN FULL!	161
A PSALM OF COMFORT	169
PRAYER OF RESTORATION	181
A SPECIAL PRAYER FOR YOU	183
ABOUT THE AUTHOR	184

ACKNOWLEDGMENTS

For those who feel hopeless toward a better life, there is no greater love than God's love for you. He sent hope through His Son Jesus Christ, who died for your sins to give you an abundant life now and forever. Receive His Gift of Love today!

To my late brother Joseph B Bristo Sr. and my nephew, Joseph Irving Bristo (only son to my beloved brother, who went home to be with the Lord on his 50th birthday, August 10, 2007.

To my dear and beloved children: Claude, Dee, Carol, Leon, Georgianna, Rebecca, and Ora D; my grandchildren and great-grandchildren. Many of the lessons contained within this book have been learned from you, my family. Therefore, I'm truly grateful that throughout all the trial and error of raising you, you still love me, Certainly, there is no stronger love one can have than family.

I would like to thank my editor, Roz A. Gee (www.rozgee.com). Without your loyalty, prayers, encouragement, and patience this project wouldn't have seen the light of day.

To my Bishop, Pastor, Spiritual Father (in Ministry) and friend, Dr. Wesley T. Cherry, Sr., of Word Alive Church International in Manassas Virginia, who loved and prayed for me and always looked beyond my faults, and saw the need. You encouraged me to be all I could be in God. You truly are a great man of God, who knew there was greatness locked within me.

To my other Spiritual Father, Pastor Kenneth Hackett of Lion of Judah Church of God in Christ in Manassas Virginia. You taught me diligently during a dark chapter of my life. "For though ye have ten thousand instructors in Christ, ye have not many fathers (I Corinthians 4:15). To you, I will be forever grateful.

Last, but certainly not least, my two daughters in the Lord: Michelle and Gwendolyn Irick. Without your prayers, love, and support during the times I wanted to give up, this book would not have been written. Thank You!

The book, ***"From the Barstool To The Pulpit"*** is a captivating autobiographical rendering of a spiritual rag to riches journey. This work chronicles the real life/real-time drama of a tremendous woman of God named Rebecca who grasped God-given purpose in the face of adversity. She was able to conquer challenges in her past by developing an unquenchable faith in God.

She is living proof that your past can "never" limit or diminish your future! As her Pastor, I can proudly declare in God that her life has become an example to many in her service to the Body of Christ. Becky's story is inextricably attached to "His"-story, which will inspire many generations to come!

Bishop Wesley T. Cherry, Sr.
Pastor, Word Alive Church International
Manassas, Virginia
www.TheWordIsAlive.com

INTRODUCTION

Allow me to unfold a story of a young girl's destiny interrupted by the fiery trials of life and God's miraculous power transforming her into a spiritually developed woman. It's a tale of triumph over all of life's mess to bring a glorious message of hope to the world!

This book is written to mothers, fathers, and all walks of life to gain a greater understanding of the importance of Salvation, and having God's wisdom operating within you. So you will be adequately prepared and equipped to rear and nurture Godly offspring—offspring who will perpetuate a God-fearing generation. Why is this critically important? It is to avoid the same costly mistakes and wave of poor choices that occurred in my life, potentially affecting your children and generations thereafter.

One may conclude, "but you made it through" after surrendering to God and His standards. However, consider the wasted seasons, years and opportunities

Introduction

that can never be regained by my own strength and power. My life's history may have been turned out differently with the proper upbringing, influence and acceptance of Christ at a younger age **(Proverbs: 22-6 & Ephesians 6:1-4).** All the misery, suffering, unwanted harvests, and bloodline curses I embraced and passed on to my children could've been revoked or even avoided altogether.

Certainly, I know our lives are not perfect, or without sorrow or heartaches **(Psalms 34:17-19).** But diligently following God's plan and provision of Salvation, along with the knowledge and understanding of His word may have caused our lives to be more purpose-driven and drama-less!

I apologized to my children for not raising them in the Lord. Although I did the best I could at the time. I regret not bringing them up according to God's standards. They were never unloved—just robbed of the knowledge that Jesus loved them. Yes, a few of my children and grandchildren are now heirs of the Kingdom. I believe that the remaining will be, in time. One thing I can attest to, since I've accepted Jesus as my personal Savior. I've tried to live a Godly life before them. They used to joke and place bets on whether Mom's "change" was real or not. But thanks unto God I've not turned back. At the printing of this book, it has been 25 years. It has not been easy, and still to this day, I have no desire to turn back. To experience and receive the gift of salvation was the "best thing" that <u>**ever**</u> happened to me. Now, they all know my born-again experience was the real deal!

God's original plan for mankind was to live in paradise and reproduce in His likeness or spiritual essence **(Genesis 1:26-31)**. Man thwarted the plan through disobedience back then and still does today. Even after the Fall **(Genesis 3:6-15)**, He made provision for us to restore fellowship with Him. We are still promised an abundant life but it's only found in Christ Jesus.

Salvation is offered to you today! If you have already received this priceless gift, then commit to a deeper relationship with Jesus, our Savior and Heavenly Father.

Introduction

May God bless, keep, comfort and heal you as you read this book!

Divine Cheers,

Evangelist Rebecca J. White

GROWING UP AND RAISING THE BAR!

Every young girl's dream used to be rather simple: grow up, get married and start a family. Well, that wasn't exactly the case for me. Today, a 21st century portrait of a childhood dream may include attending an Ivy League school, achieving corporate executive status, owning investment property and maybe tying the knot and planning a family before age 40! Boy, our world has changed and so have our dreams. From my earliest memories, when the question was asked, "What do you want to be when you grow up?" I would quickly answer a Private Secretary making plenty of money, wearing beautiful clothing and living in a Boss *(fine)* home. No children were included in my dream at the time. For the record, at the writing of this book I was never employed as a Private Secretary. However, I did attend business school and became a Bank Check Proof Operator and Department Supervisor. On the west side of Philadelphia is where I grew up, along with my favorite hero in the whole wide world, my big brother Joseph affectionately known as "Joe B." We lived in a three-story apartment building on the first floor with my great aunt and her mother, who we all called "Big Momma."

Too young to register for school, I stayed at home with Big Momma and we spent our days keeping one another company. I have fond memories of running my hands through her long wavy, silver hair making an amateur attempt at hair braiding. Big Momma was mixed with Cherokee Indian. My folks were natives of Louisiana. Thus my heritage is a fusion of bloodlines like so many in this country. The hues of our skin ran from light bright to Café `Ole to a beautiful dark blend like premium roasted coffee. The mix of skin tones and high cheekbones didn't seem to affect me at all. My world was small during this time and the faces I saw everyday were part of the norm. My brother and I, along with the rest of the family listened to shows like The Lone Ranger, and his faithful companion Tonto. Come on, can't you just hear the announcer saying "Hi `OOOO Silver, the Lone Ranger and his faithful companion Tonto." By the way, Tonto was an American Indian same as Big Momma's bloodline. We used to also watch the Amos and Andy Show. My mother loved the daytime drama shows. Back in the day, they were sponsored by soap detergent companies, which the modern name "Soap Opera" may have been derived. Some things do not change after all eh?

Our family started to expand with my Aunt introducing us to a stream of "Uncles." First was Uncle Bates who was a very pleasant person. His presence made our house seemed more like a family. I liked his grey hair and beard that reminded me of Uncle Remus *(character from one of the black folklore tales, often read to us.)* Uncle Bates purchased the first family automobile. It had running boards along the doors. I loved jumping on those running boards while the automobile was in slow motion. On Sundays, we'd all hop in to ride over to New Jersey. I don't recall going over a bridge as is today. We rolled onto a ferryboat that took us from Philadelphia to New Jersey. We'd visit our real Uncle Lew *(my aunt's brother)* who lived in a peaceful, countryside community called Magnolia. He served in the Army stationed at Fort Dix. The first in our family to buy a home, this allowed for many cozy visits. All of his army buddies could now hang out in the city and the country. Uncle Lew married Mary, who hailed from our native home of Louisiana. Aunt Mary had a sister named Jane and boy, she was wise beyond her years *(at least I thought so!)* Around 10 years old, I was becoming curious about some things being whispered within our house but never explained. However, Ms. Jane and her frisky friends were willing to tell it all. I learned more than I needed to know on those New Jersey summer retreats. Mom sent me there to keep me from the evils of the big city. While there, we'd pick blueberries, strawberries and have picnic lunches of fried chicken with all the trimmings. These were some of the treasured years of my childhood.

One cousin, Eddie, was also stationed at Fort Dix. He made frequent pop in visits on the weekends. He'd bring friends and they would drink and party to no end. One weekend, he arrived with a fellow solider named Robert, who later became my stepfather. My folks were no different than most colored folk in the late 40's and early 50's—hard working Southerners who migrated north from slavery and sharecropping oppression. Weekend partying was their way of letting off steam from a hard weeks work, trying to make a better life up north. On the second floor of our apartment building lived a couple and their adult son—Mrs. Beneva, Mr. Benny, and Henry. Boy! Our neighbors were always getting drunk and fighting every weekend like clock work. You could always predict the police showing up to calm things down and restore order. In those days, not many went to jail for this type of domestic disturbance. Police considered this normal behavior from our kind of people. At this stage of my life this was the only acceptable dysfunction I was exposed to. By Monday morning, the dust finally settled down stairs and upstairs—no more drinking and partying. It was time to get back to the work grind of 8-40 *(8 hour day, 40 hour week)*.

To supplement our income my mother became a neighborhood number writer (*bookie*). She along with my Aunt present employment included pressing shirts at a local laundry. Mom's boyfriend Mack introduced her to this illegal activity. Every 'hood had a top man and Mack was our lead guy. My mother became his chief underwriter. Everyone played "numbers", an illegal form of gambling, which was very lucrative as long as the police didn't catch you. Everyone had a "pet number" that was sure to hit on the day the bet was placed with their bookie. The winning numbers were based on the local horse race winning. Mom did well and while we never lacked for any material thing her social status increased. Eventually, she became the club president of the Social Steppers. They threw lavish cabarets, card and house parties. Additional occasions for drinking and gambling that ruled the nights like an iron fist. Often times, I remember waking up at night and watching my mother remove combs from her long upsweep hairdo. Bills of various dominations would fall where she stashed the night's gain from Pity Pat and other card game winnings. These were exciting and happy days. No worries! An apartment vacancy became available on the third floor of our building. Mom was able to secure that unit for us. Oh happy day for my brother and me—we shared a bedroom while my mom had her own. Yes, we were all in one living space. Although crowded, we didn't mind because we were family!

SHATTERED GLASSES AND BROKEN DREAMS

After moving upstairs, things began to change for us. Mom was off to work. Joe B. was in school and doing whatever teenage boys did in the 50's. When he was not busy being the man of the house *(mom left him in charge when she wasn't there, and of course he thought he was The Boss.)* Perhaps that's why we had so many fights! He loved to tease his little sister *(hence my nick name Sister)*. Our routine fighting caused Mom to constantly buy new windowpanes. Windows were always broken because I hurled any *available* object at Joe's head and of course, he would duck. Pow! There goes another pane. Mom grew tired of punishing us for the same crime through our squabbles wouldn't last for long. During the summer, Joe and I would sleep on the rooftop by climbing out of our kitchen window and sleep peacefully all night. This was our outdoor air conditioning. Happy, happy days!

Mack, the chief bookie, was no longer on the scene. Mom began to date cousin Eddie's friend, Robert. My brother and I didn't know anything about him except he'd party hard with our folks when Eddie came over to visit. He became a father figure and treated me special. This was a foreign yet exciting experience because prior to this time, male interaction within our family structure primarily consisted of just being cordial to little girls. With the exception of my big brother who always treated me exceptional—he was my father, friend, and hero all wrapped up into one! Now, Robert was present to take me for walks, buy me candy, and pay special attention to my mom and me. Yes, I'd say I liked this guy but don't remember my brother being involved much while Robert was visiting (*Wells of Wisdom: For Parents Only section.*) This new male relationship may have contributed to why things went so terribly wrong in his life.

Several weeks later, there was a great scurrying throughout the entire apartment building. I had no earthly idea a wedding was about to take place! There, my mother stood in a pale blue wedding dress about to marry Robert. Wow, I had a Daddy now and we operated as a family unit although Aunt Lisa, Big Momma, and Uncle Nate were still on the first floor. Some of the partying and drinking slowed down now that Mom had a new husband. He was still in the Army so we basically saw him while on military leave which varied. Mom still worked long hours while Joe B. and I adjusted to our new life of having a man around. In the beginning things were fine but Joe B. eventually became a belligerent young man, which was out of character for him. He resented having another man around stealing the affection and attention he was used to getting. Perhaps in his mind, these were his women folk. Who was this guy he hardly knew to intrude his kingdom and take over? One thing for sure, my hero was getting into increased trouble with Mom and at school. **This generally happens when no true bonding takes place in the home unit...beware!** Mom wasn't prepared for when she found herself in a gridlocked battle between her man and son. During these tug-of-wars, Mom kept contact with her best friends, Dena and Zemmett, a couple she'd known for quite some time. I suppose she needed space from time to time since Robert was away on active duty. In addition, she remained active with the Social Steppers and played cards. Dena and Zemmett would often accompany her to these games and that meant they were at the house frequently. Joe B. was seldom around anymore and I learned to entertain myself with my favorite pastime—playing store. Next to one of the large windows, I'd place a wide board next to the wall and my bed. I'd line up my dishes, dolls and other toy items pretending to sell them to inanimate customers. While I enjoyed this, it was the beginning of God teaching me how to walk alone and be content.

My body began to develop without me taking much notice. When you are a happy young girl and no one to educate you on the natural stages of development, you grow up oblivious of what others may notice. I started to become uncomfortable with the gestures of some. For instance, Zemmett use to tickle me all the time. One day it didn't feel right and immediately I didn't like it anymore. I didn't know how to make him stop because in those days children were seen and not heard. Even if you were in physical pain, if there were no visible wounds nothing was considered wrong. I suffered from terrible backaches but I was told "your back can't be hurting when all you have is gristle!" No one took seriously that my reoccurring pain was most likely from being struck by cars three different times (yes, you read that correctly, three!) The devil had a hit out on my life even then. I believe the Lord blessed me with the wisdom to stop reacting when Zemmett tickled me. Thus, he wouldn't have an excuse to put his hands all over me. Unfortunately, I knew if I spoke up about how I was feeling I wouldn't have been believed. Honestly, I wouldn't have known how to explain it if I dared to speak up. My lack of response and reaction ended my first encounter of being subtly taken advantaged of. Dena, mom's best friend developed some sort of illness, which required surgery and she was afraid. I heard them discussing her fears. Mom encouraged her to go through with it, assuring her everything would be all right. The night before surgery would be her last visit with us. Upon leaving, I recall her final words as she stood on the staircase; "Dora D (my mother) this is the last time I will ever leave your house." it was a self-fulfilling prophecy because when she died on the operating table. This left a huge void in my mother's life for Dena. They were like peas in a pod. Life went on, meanwhile Zemmett's visits discontinued and I said good riddance!

SIN ON THE ROCKS

Joe B. was constantly getting into more trouble, but he was still considered my superhero. Prior to leaving for several years, he came to my defense against an ice delivery boy. We owned an icebox, as there weren't any frost-free refrigerators during this era. We lived around the corner from the icehouse and one day after placing an order; this wild child thought he could have his way with me. I didn't have a clue why he was all over me trying to force me to the floor so I started screaming and fighting with all of my might. So loudly until he thought twice of his intended dirty deed. Running all the way home in sheer terror, I told Joe B. about the attack. He headed around the corner like a missile and I was on his tail. He beat the perpetrator "good fashion" as the older folk used to say. There was no more trouble from that kid—he finally "cooled" off. ☺

A new addition was on the way—mom announced she was having a baby. This would be my stepfather's first child—the year was 1948. As a result, more lifestyle changes I had to accept. Mom was often sick, and Joe B. was away serving in the Army. He found himself in so much trouble; the authorities were threatening to send him to reform school. If you were 16 years of age or older, you were basically given two choices: reform school or the Armed Services. So he left for several years between occasional visits while on leave. Boy, did I miss him terribly. In 1949, my brand new sister showed up and took center stage.

Isn't she lovely? Well, not quite. She dominated the entire house, screeching and hollering day and night. I tried to adjust—perhaps if I wasn't forced into the position to help care of her. Gee whiz, I was only a young girl myself! I didn't want to constantly change diapers, feed and bathe a newborn. All of this was overwhelming because before the [real] baby, there were only my dolls and myself. My dolls never cried, crapped or needed to be fed *(only to spit up all over me later, phew!)* No doubt, this little suckling was an invader on my small planet. Oh why did she have to show up now? Woe was I. Surely, I was acting like a selfish, spoiled brat but that's what happens when siblings are not properly prepared to welcome and receive new family members. No one in my family knew much about that sort of stuff; my folk came from a generation of sharecroppers. But as time progressed, I accepted the position as Big Sister as she began to grow.

My first day of school, trust me, didn't go well. Settling and adjusting to a brand new environment and classroom setting, I'd arrive at home and find my precious dolls and toys demolished by Baby Terminator. She was now in the crawling, reaching up and pulling down stage. My love and tolerance continued to decline as I pondered why how did she get here in the first place. Let me pause to clarify that my sister and I enjoy a loving relationship today, thanks be unto God. In fact, at the writing of this book and after years of living several states apart, she has relocated to Virginia where we live only 12 miles from one another. We are having a blast reconnecting and I appreciate the moments and memories we're treasuring. A level of normalcy was slowly coming into view. My new dad was returning home on leave more often and there were fewer battles with my little sister. Our apartment was overcrowded so my aunt and mother decided to pool money together to buy a house on the southwest side of town. Big Momma tagged along too!

For my age, I was a rather large girl that was rapidly developing—budding breasts, spreading hips, and protruding buttocks. If Mother Nature had asked my opinion, I wouldn't be in agreement at all. The opposite sex began noticing me. I, however, didn't know the significance of what was happening. Again, no one explained the various stages of adolescence to me. Mother wanted to saddle me in a bra and girdle much to my terror. The bra felt like I was being squeezed breathless. The girdle was made of skin-sucking rubber and baby powder was used just to pull it up! Once home, I would anxiously free myself of these undergarments.

By now, we had been in our new residence long enough to have settled and prepare for yep, you guessed it, another baby. Arriving would be a bouncing boy this time. Now we were back to being overcrowded because the place only had two bedrooms—Auntie had the front room all to herself. We remained there and eventually our family consisted of Mom, Dad, three little ones and me. As more children kept coming, so did my chores and responsibilities. I was moved from a bunk bed to a pallet *(bed made of quilts)* on the floor. This became a breeding ground for sexual perversion— where molestation began in that back bedroom. Late in the night, my stepfather would slip into my bed and slide his hands in my underwear fondling my genitals. What does an innocent young girl do or say? I had no clue what was actually occurring being paralyzed by fear and completely disassociated with awakened sensations I couldn't identify with. These unwanted invasions took place from time to time. I suppose whenever he felt his deeds would remain undetected, he took advantage. I never protested or muttered a word knowing I'd never be believed. Even if I had the courage, I wouldn't even know how to explain what was happening to me. He spent a lot of time scheming for his perpetrations. My innocence was being snatched with my unwitting cooperation.

Reflecting on all the loving fatherly attention received when growing up; at times I got into trouble doing the usual mischievous things. Once I lied about playing with matches and my stepfather saw me. He then told my mother I was lying when asked about it. No, he never stopped me but instead used this incident for leverage to build a strong defense against me. Even upon telling the truth, I'd never be believed by mother again especially if *he said* I was lying. **Parents beware—this is the typical profile of a pedophile. They ingratiate themselves with a child and become a trusted family member if they aren't already. So that their integrity would never be questioned if ever accused**. I couldn't even tell Big Momma who was growing old by now.

One night there was a great commotion going on downstairs in the room where Big Momma slept. Turned out she was having some kind of attack or seizure which resulted in her death. My last memory was my stepfather and mother leaning over her as she gasped for breath while the attendants wheeled her out on a gurney. Next time I saw her was in a coffin at her funeral. Having no concept of death, I screamed for her to wake up and get out of that box but to no avail. Suddenly, life was sad, as there was no one now to receive motherly hugs and warm kisses from. My mother was not an affectionate person though she loved us in her own way.

Those unwanted nighttime visitations didn't stop. The fondling escalated to intimate rubbing and arousing, feelings that were now pleasurable. Being masturbated by this monster shouldn't have been happening to a young girl or any girl for that matter, especially in the same room where my mother, brothers and sister were all sleeping! Thank God, there was never a penetration. Shortly thereafter, my menstrual period began. My mother explained that now I was a woman capable of having babies. But that meant nothing to me except another annoyance I had to put up with. I was shown how to put on a sanitary napkin and given a serious warning, "Don't play with boys because you will get pregnant!" Yep, I was the dumbest girl on the schoolyard. Besides, we always played with boys at recess and on many occasions, I went home crying believing I was going to have a baby. ☺

My stepfather's lewd behavior continued until he contracted some sort of illness and was transferred to a hospital away from the family for an eighteen-month period. I don't know if his excessive drinking had anything to do with his condition. He could down a fifth *(whiskey)* before inhaling the next breath. When you're used to the stuff brewed in the back woods stills *(i.e. corn whiskey),* store bought products must have been tame to the taste. In his absence, things were normal in our household. Mom worked and I took my sister to school, assumed more chores, watched the adult's party and got down on the weekends too. Becoming lonely, I desired friends who were closer to my age. The girls I wanted to befriend were much older and I clung to a young lady who lived down the street. Seemingly, every night some one needed something from the store. Nightly, I would stop by so she could walk to the store with me. I would wait even when she took her time to come out the house. Needless to say, I got into trouble for taking so long.

Guess, I was looking for love. Love came up short for me because at my house, it certainly wasn't a luxury or even standard. One evening during one of my store runs, I was attacked by a pack of dogs *(they were allowed to roam in packs back then.)* Never knew I could run so fast or jump a fence so high. While on another store run, a posse of boys pulled me into an alley to pull a train *(gang rape)* on me. I fought that night with the strength of Samson; I knew God was with me. That's when I decided it was worth waiting for my friend to walk with me. Perhaps you are thinking…why didn't she just tell her mother what was happening on these store runs? Glad you asked. It would've been either perceived as an excuse for not wanting to go or good old-fashioned fear. Then I would be interrogated on what I did to cause these events and lectured on if I'd been where I was supposed to be, none of this would've happened. Where, oh where was my big brother Joe B., my protector?

My friendship came to a screeching halt as she and her beau got married. There was no room for a pesky, little sister friend any longer. A few of mom's friends from across town found their way to our new hood. One in particular was a little mentally impaired. He sold newspapers to supplement his income because he still lived at home. But somehow he found himself becoming attached to me and I didn't encourage his interest because it didn't seem right, period. In fact, I was beginning to be uneasy with gaining attention from the opposite sex.

My stepfather returned home from his 18-month sabbatical, Mom and my siblings were happy at his return. I'm sure I was too but I don't fully recall. He brought transfer orders for overseas duty with him. The news flashed like a bolt of lighting. My family was packing up to move away but I didn't and begged Mom to stay stateside with my Aunt *(huge mistake)*. Mom consented. I figured this was my big chance to stop being the live-in maid/babysitter to my mom and siblings. **Parents don't have a bunch of kids and make your oldest or older children primarily responsible for their care and keep. Trust me, they will come to resent you for it.** It was my job to take care of them when I got home from school. Mom went back to work and Emmett showed back up with a new woman who babysat until I arrived home. A rather lazy lady, I'd say, who left dirty dishes in the sink and kept a messy house. Therefore it was added to my job description to have everything cleaned by the time Mom arrived. Even my walk from school was spoiled by having to watch my baby sister safely home. These caused me to get into neighborhood fights because kids liked to pull her long braids. One huge fight resulted in my opponents' clothing being beaten off—talk about a neighborhood show-n-tell! ☺

STIRRING UP LOVE

By now I had a fully developed body likes a grown woman and men were noticing me for all the wrong reasons. Left in my aunt's care ended my childhood and put me on a fast track introduction into adulthood. My aunt was supposed to use the monies sent by my mom for my support. To this day, I don't know how much was used for that reason. All I ever saw was fifteen dollars a month. Out of which I was suppose to pay for school transportation *(Junior High school),* lunch, clothes and school supplies. Demand was high and supply was low. I landed a job as a nanny on the weekends and during the summer at the shore. Of course, I lied and told the lady I was older. At age twelve, I was in full bloom. After all, at least I was getting paid to be a slave now! This worked out fine until my boss' unruly children (who I was not allowed to discipline, by the way) grew out of control. I quit during that summer and came home.

My aunt had several beaus on rotation—some nice and others weren't. One in particular, I really disliked because he always tried to rule over me so we always clashed. By now, my aunt and I were on very bad terms; she was stealing my money and verbally abusive daily. My aunt's preferred words to me were, "Little Bastard." **Parents, this is another no-no. I despise that word today. Even when I was habitually cursing I never used it.** To top it off, the last thing I needed was some low life dude making matters worse in my life. One day in the heat of anger, I threatened to take a hammer to his head and after that I had no more trouble from him.

The search for love, kindness, affection and attention were my top priorities. Wherever they were, I just knew that they weren't in my house. Subsequently, I began to hang out with a neighborhood girl who would talk about "doing it" with boys. She and her family professed being religious and I studied Catholicism with them.

In my quest for love, I became weary of the traditional Baptist Church. I was made to go like most kids but saw no benefit in being there. The same people I saw shouting, singing, and dancing on Sunday mornings were the same ones drinking and partying with my folks on Saturday night. **Parents know that your children will watch and emulate your behavior. Remember, they live with you 24/7.** So when I had the chance to go to church with my Catholic neighbors *(satisfying mom)* and stay for an hour *(no dressing up, no one passing out on me)*, I begged to go.

This unholy alliance, however, would lead down a path and lifestyle I would later live to regret. Under her tutelage, there were conversations on how good "doing it" was. Unfortunately, like a sheep being led to the slaughter, I followed. She made it all sound so wonderful *(the devil always does.)* There was a boy at school who was interested in me. So we arranged to meet for our first date when my aunt wouldn't be at home. I was scared out of my wits and was totally clueless. We fondled for about a hot minute and all of a sudden I sent him packing. The poor boy was knocking on my door for weeks. I ignored him until he finally gave up hope. Whew, thank goodness! Afterwards, I started to hang out next door with the Hughes' family who had an older teen girl, Linda. They treated me with a love I felt was genuine. Wrong again! They ran a speakeasy *(after-hours joint)* where booze was sold and women and rooms were for rent. My sex education went up several notches. I would spend the night in their home for the company. I must have been marked "vulnerable" because their daughter began to masturbate me when I fell asleep. Again, I felt violated and trapped.

Hanging out with the Hughes and their bi-sexually active daughter, was the last place I needed to be at this age and stage of my life. Pandora's Box was now opened—I learned how to serve liquor, food, and act like an older, mature woman. None of the men who visited the establishment were ever allowed to go out-of-bounds with me. Thank goodness, Mrs. Hughes kept them in line but she had no control over her own daughter. The crowd Linda associated with was a group of sex-crazed teens in Catholic school and there was one mannish bull-dike *(butch or lesbian)* who probably influenced Linda toward female seduction, which she tried to practice on me. Although the enemy tried to distort my natural desire for the opposite sex, thank you Jesus that it didn't work! For the record, these were my only encounters with this illicit behavior with another female and I was a fearful and unwilling participant.

During these days, I was exposed to a lot of lascivious behavior that would affect my future. There was a boy named Jimmy, who lived on the street adjacent to ours. I thought he was so cute. I made sure I kept myself in his view whenever possible. By now I was going to bars, yes bars, and getting served. The legal age was 21 but Linda taught me how to dress to look older, so I accompanied her and her male friends on various dates. Her butch tendencies began to dissipate. Girlfriend discovered the real thing! ☺ Across town, we'd sit in bars and sip whiskey and ginger ale with the soldier boys who frequented her parent's speakeasy. I was drinking often by now. After all, I'd been around the stuff and this behavior all my life. No one discouraged me from this behavior, so one thing led to the next. Hanging out with adults and acting like one—you wanted to do what they did. When Jimmy came knocking and begging, I said sure I'm game. All the fluff my girlfriend told me about how good it would feel along with the intimate gestures I saw among those who I knew were having sex. I figured it was about time I got some loving too! Whoa, I wasn't prepared for what would happen in my aunt's back bedroom. Spirits of lust were lurking around to attach themselves through my curiosity.

When Jimmy mounted me to steal my virginity—yes I say steal though I was a willing participant. For I now know it was stolen as surely as if I had been raped. Upon penetration, I screamed and tried to push him off because of the extreme pain. Prior to this, I'd never been penetrated but his battery was fully charged and he wasn't about to stop this train. By the way, Linda left out the part about the pain of your hymen being torn! ***The purpose of this precious, thin layer of mucous membrane guards the entry way to a woman's vagina. It should be available to offer to her husband on their wedding night sealing a covenant between a man and woman. No greater gift or prize can a man be offered in knowing the purity of his new bride. God planned it as such so that the act of lovemaking (not mere sex) would tie two individuals on a greater physical and spiritual level (Proverbs 5:18, 19 and Hebrews 13:4).*** This was not what I expected and no pleasure was experienced in my book. To my relief *literally*, we were interrupted because my aunt came home unexpectedly. I was afraid of being caught so I was finally able to get him to stop and dash out the back window. Our irresponsible behavior resulted in a seed being planted and my becoming pregnant with my first child. We never got together again, even though I thought he was cute but I guess the, "I've got what I want from you, so see ya!" mindset kicked in. **Take notes young ladies: A teen pregnancy was the result of a seed planted and the harvest it produced.** I foolishly told my so-called friend, Linda, what happened. She couldn't wait to spread the news through out the hood like wild fire. Another friendship came to a screeching halt because another person had betrayed me again I thought I could trust. Immediately, every young and old rascal propositioning me as if I had a sign on my back that read, "I'm yours for the asking." Even Mr. Hughes from next door showed up at my house saying how safe it would be "to take a dip from his ship" since he was sterile and there was no chance I'd get pregnant. Ha, too late! Honestly, I was too stupid to know what I'd done and now my reputation was ruined. Every encounter I had with a boy after that, I was expected to put out. Some I did and others I didn't because I was still looking for love. I didn't know the difference between love and lust. When you've never been loved properly, your reality of it becomes warped. You desire it so badly until you give yourself to anyone who will show you any affection. This is how so many young people end up on the trash heap of life, when the adults responsible for your upbringing, fail you in the love department.

CHEERS, FEARS AND TEARS

Months before I began to show, I kept going out drinking and having sex. It never dawned on me that I was pregnant and in junior high school. I was a teenager by day and thought of as a sex object by night. I don't remember when the realization occurred to me. When it did, I was scared and confused. How could this have happened to me? I didn't know what to do or expect for I was still living at home with my aunt. When she found out, I was put out! So I ended up next door at the Hughes'. Welcomed with open arms, Rita *(Mrs. Hughes)* saw an opportunity to seize a young unwed mothers' baby since she was unable to have children. However, the first thing she made me do was to write my mother overseas and inform her of my pregnancy. This was the hardest letter I've ever written knowing she would be heartbroken and severely disappointed. No matter what, I always wanted to please my mother. It was decided that I would remain stateside until the rest of my family returned. I had to quit school in the ninth grade because there were no schools or programs for unwed mothers in that day. There was no such thing as you attending high school with a protruding belly. There was no public acceptance, only shame and embarrassment for you and your family. Many girls were sent south for delivery to avoid controversy. The months leading to my delivery were a challenge—body swells, morning sickness, clinic visits, and doctors poking me inside and out. Not to mention, buying ugly maternity clothes, and serving in the house to earn my right to stay there.

My long, lost big brother came back into my life and was disappointed to find out that I was pregnant. We began to establish our relationship on a more adult level now. He gotten married and introduced me to his new wife. She was sweet and I liked her right away. It was so fun to visit them. Adele never shook a wagging finger in my "fifteen year- old face." I think that's why I liked her because she was just so full of love for everyone. Joe B. and Adele had a cute little boy named after him and it wasn't long before they were expecting their second child. Meanwhile, Joe B. had gotten into some kind of trouble and was incarcerated. I don't think he ever knew she was pregnant. When I received the news she was hospitalized, I was stunned to see her in such a horrible condition. Her bed was in a room where oxygen tanks were stored. Adele was weak, feverish and her lips were blistered and crusted with blood. Barely able to speak, she began to unfold all that led up her present condition. I listened in disbelief as she described how her mother, who she loved dearly, convinced her to have an abortion. Unfortunately, the procedure went horribly wrong. Her mom wasn't fond of my brother and thought her daughter shouldn't have another baby by him. Since my brother was incarcerated, I suppose she felt helpless, and defenseless against her mother's reasoning and influence. Infection set in Adele's body from head to toe. I don't know how long it was before her family sought medical help, but when they did it was too late. Holding me near her mouth, she made me promise not to tell my brother what really happened. I've kept that promise to this day, even though he's deceased.

As I made that vow, I found myself shaking and crying uncontrollably until I ended up leaving the hospital wondering how I would cope with this news. After all, I was just fifteen and pregnant with my first child. I had so many questions as to how could a mother, especially one who was a professing Catholic and registered nurse; allow such a thing to happen to an unborn child. Shortly thereafter, Adele died and my brother and I were devastated. He had no other family to support him during this time besides me. The rest of our family was still overseas. On the evening of the funeral, there was a violent March snow storm occurring. Soggy, wet snow and ice, downed utility lines everywhere making it extremely precarious to walk. Joe B. was released from incarceration for the services. To tell you the truth, I don't know how we got through this time; it must have been God's grace and mercy. Joe B. not knowing how or why his wife was suddenly gone. And I was tormented with the secrecy of the real reason for the cause of her death.

After the burial, Joe B. returned to his world and exited my life *(once again)* not to be seen or heard from for several years. Within two weeks, I gave birth to my first child in the same hospital where Adele died. My options were narrow in that I had no choice but to continue receiving assistance from the Hughes'. All the precious hopes and memories I had of Joe B. and I being together slowly dissipated. Labor was imminent as I was abruptly waken by a sudden pain in my lower back and abdomen area, which I deemed to be gas. I rolled over and went back to sleep. The next one was severe enough to wake up the entire household. Now there was a consensus that it was just gas, so I was given cola to bring it up. Well, it was brought up all right—right before everyone's faces as I began to upchuck. The pains began to occur more often and intensely. Suddenly, there was a new consensus as they realized I was in labor! Someone called a cab to transport me to the hospital.

The sudden attack I felt was like no other pain before. Even menstrual cramps were never like this! I squeezed Rita's hand so hard she thought I'd broken it. **Never hold the hand of a woman who's in labor!** My occasional groans became full blasted screams and I do mean full blasted. The attending nurse spoke these unforgettable words to me, "Honey you might as well stop screaming. Every time you do, you are bringing the baby back up. The same way it went in is the same way it's coming out. Now start panting like a dog." Why on earth did she tell me that? I really screamed even the more. I assumed they were going to put me to sleep and "cut" the baby out. I wasn't educated or informed on anything regarding the stages of being pregnant let alone the labor and delivery process. After a horrific, 8-hour labor ordeal, I became the 15 year-old mother of a bouncing baby boy. Was I ready for this? No. But the reality was, I'm now in an adult situation I'd brought on myself through promiscuous behavior.

The next two days were pure hell. I was in a large ward where your babies were beside you. There were no private or semi-private rooms and basically, you were responsible for taking care of them right after birth no matter how you felt. Being new to the process of post-birth, I was forced to get up with a stitch-filled bottom and afterbirth pains to care for my newborn infant. Observing my struggle, an older woman suggested I smoke a cigarette to help curb the pain. *(There is always someone present to entice you toward greater self-destruction.)* I took her up on her offer and began what turned into a twenty-six year habit. Thank God for deliverance today! *(1 Corinthians 6:19, 20)*

REMOVIN' THE BLACK LABEL

My newborn son and I arrived back at the Hughes residence. We tried to settle in, but it was tough. Their place wasn't a proper environment for children period, let alone a teen, unwed mother. Soon, living conditions began to go awry. He cried during the night, awaking everyone from their sleep *(except Mr. Hughes who worked at night.)* He spat up constantly and a strange infestation of bed bugs didn't help matters at all. Many nights I spent awake to keep the bugs off my baby boy while trying to keep him quiet as long as possible. Half asleep during the day, I'd scrub his stained cloth diapers and clothes in the bathtub on a rub board. I was thankful when the spring months came with fair weather so clothes could dry easily. Imagine hanging wet clothes out to dry in the freezing cold and watching them freeze along with your fingers sticking to the clothespins. After about three weeks, I couldn't take it any more. Finally, I humbled myself and asked my aunt if I could come home because enough was enough. At least there were no bugs in her house but my stay didn't last long because I couldn't tolerate her boy friend. Another I ended up confronting with a hammer until he understood I meant business and backed off. Once my dear aunt learned about the confrontation, she put the baby and me out—without our clothes, his formula or extra bottles. I walked the streets for hours with my baby. Nightfall was fast approaching and I only had one bottle, no diapers and no place to call home.

The Hughes' allowed me to come back but there was a hidden motive because Rita really wanted my baby. This was partially why I left before. There was constant pressure for her to raise him with me being unmarried and so young. Although I knew what she was saying made sense, it just wasn't right for me. I didn't know how I would take care of my son, but I new I was not going to give him away because he was mine! He was someone I could love like I'd never been loved. Shortly thereafter, we received notice that my family would be returning stateside. I didn't know what to expect now that I had a three-month old. As it turned out, mother didn't arrive soon enough to rescue me from another bad choice. I entered a new relationship with one of the military guys who frequented the Hughes' house. I was extremely lonely and unsure of any future with anyone. Oh, this guy was different though. He treated me like he really cared about me. He knew I had a child and because he thought I was much older, he expected sex to be part of our relationship. I didn't disappoint him and at least he was gentle.

My parents graciously accepted their new grandchild with opened arms. No speeches or quarrels like I expected. Instead we discussed how my son and I would be taken care of. My stepfather wanted to know who the daddy was and why he hadn't stepped up to the plate. When I discovered I was with child and informed Mr. James (*Jimmy*) McNeil, he said he needed to *discuss* this with his mother. **Caution young ladies because it's obvious I had chosen a boy and not a man. He didn't need to <u>discuss</u> jumping in the sack with me!** Anyway, after his discussion, his mother said, "Her son couldn't possibly be the father because I was too BLACK." He and his family were high yellow folks. So she just knew her son couldn't possibly think about bringing home a BLACK gal as a potential daughter-in-law. Oh, the family would never accept such a thing. Come on people you know: momma's baby and daddy's maybe! In the late fifties, there was no black pride but we were in the generation of the 'N' word and colored people. Dark-skinned folk felt inferior and thought we needed a light-skinned person to validate us. In fact, this was a popular saying, "If you were white, you were right. If you were brown, you could stick around. If you were yellow, you could get a fellow but if you were black, you had to get back." Negative mindsets like this can and still heavily influence a generation **(Proverbs 18:21).** I passed on his mother's message to my stepfather and to my surprise he was infuriated. He sent me to fetch this young man to stand before him and plead his case. He violated his daughter and produced an offspring, therefore an acknowledgement or confirmation was warranted and this wasn't a request but a demand. I got the same response, "I need to talk to my momma."

By this time Jimmy had seen the baby who, as God would have it, arrived looking just like his daddy, same color and all. He knew the child was his. When he finally did appear before my step dad the message from his momma was, "My mother said what would be cheaper to give you money for the child or marry her?" My dad became so angry, he told him to go tell his momma, "Neither one—he would take care of us both." Well, that was the end of that. I was never more proud of him than on that day. It was like having my big brother Joe protecting me again. For many years, I neither saw nor heard from Jimmy or his momma.

BLOODY MARY OR BLOODY BECKY

Mother left the country with four children and returned with five. Now, we all shared a bedroom in the same cramped apartment but this time, I wasn't being molested anymore. And my aunt had a big change of heart once my family returned. My stepfather had been on extended leave since returning stateside. The Vietnam War was in effect by now and he received orders to ship out. Before leaving, he decided to secure a bigger and better home for his expanded family, which consisted of five children, I made six. This concludes my exodus from Philadelphia to New Jersey. We settled in a community called Somerville. It featured brand new, sand and stucco, two-story homes with three bedrooms and a porch. I was blown away with the brand new, shiny appliances, wall-to-wall carpet, hardwood floors and a huge basement with gas heat, which meant no more stoking a coal burning furnace. Hallelujah! Mother was happy to have her own home. We settled in and my step dad was shipped off to Nam, Things were smooth for a while. We meet a new military family who moved next door to us. Consequently, it wasn't long before the partying started up with our new friends. By now Mom knew I was smoking and drinking.

Deon, the nice military guy, was discharged from the service and came looking for me. Somehow he found me in Jersey and I ended up pregnant again. We didn't make any immediate plans but he did come to see me and off and on. We sort of drifted apart before the birth of our daughter who was premature, by the way. I made it through the delivery while nurturing of a sick infant with my mothers help. I didn't see Deon again for almost two years. During that time, I became involved with a married man, an experience that resulted in a real heartbreak. He left town with a promise to send for me and mine, but I guess the pressure put on him by his wife and family prevailed. To add to the drama, I became pregnant with his child. Yes, round three, pregnant again in my quest for love and settling for lust. **This is the result of what happens when you cannot discern the difference between lust and love in relationships**. Of course, this was too much for him especially after a recent altercation between his wife and me. I ended up in court and being humiliated beyond words. Sin will bring you down low. He had decided to follow his brother and move out west. After settling there, he sent for his wife, who was also pregnant. I discovered this through another humiliating scene in a grocery line as she boasted loudly about being sent for by her husband. **Sin will take you further than you want to go and make you pay more than you can ever imagine.**

Deon showed back up in my life. I suppose you could say he rescued me because with three kids now this guy still wanted to marry me. Yes, I will repeat that. Someone wanted to marry me and in my mind, all my sorrows would now be over. As fate would have it, I was just eighteen and needed my mother's signature, which she refused to do. Why, who knows? Attempting to go out of state didn't work for us either; however, he was determined to have me. To show how serious he was, he went and purchased a home in Philadelphia. We settled into a nice three-bedroom home on the west side. Besides having to compromise on used furniture, life was pretty good. After a couple of months, with the pressure of being six months pregnant, with his child, and a little one who suffered from separation anxiety *(screaming uncontrollably when I was out of her sight)*, two toddlers, and Deon's demanding and possessive ways were more than I could handle. I recall sitting on the porch in the evenings to talk to my new neighbor. A few minutes would pass and I would be summoned back inside to watch sports with him. He wanted all my attention once the children and evening chores were finished. I felt encased and only released to serve and attend those around me. Toward the latter months of pregnancy being heavy with child, I wasn't allowed to leave an unwashed dish in the sink or break away for some private time. The demands were draining the very life out of me. One night we had a big blow up about a dish being left unwashed and that was the straw that broke with camel's back. I called my mother and asked if I could come home with my children. Deon was left to fend on his own. Ironically, he didn't try to stop us when the cab arrived to take us back to New Jersey.

By now, my own Mom was pregnant and due soon. Her husband was away on active duty so I just slipped back into the role of Chief Caretaker again. I'll never forget the night Mom went into labor though—it was unforgettable. No one was around we knew who owned a car. She needed to go to the military hospital in Philadelphia. After searching the neighborhood frantically, I found a lady who was willing to take a chance and drive us there. She hadn't driven in several years. I know the Lord was with us that night! While trying to direct an unsure, nervous driver across a bridge to another state, Mom began to cry out in pain and hemorrhage in my lap as the baby was attempting to make its way into the world. But something was going very wrong. Upon arrival, the emergency team met us at the door. They didn't know which one of us was the patient. I was bloody from my waist down. We put Mom on the gurney and they rolled her away to the delivery room. The driver, our kind friend left soon thereafter. Who could blame her? I sat for what seemed like hours waiting for a status of her condition. Finally a doctor appeared with news that mom and baby would be fine. What a relief! I can't imagine what my Mother went through that night but she was never the same afterwards. By now, we were in the wee hours of the morning and I had to make my way back to New Jersey. It suddenly dawned on me how far out of bounds I was from the train station. There were no cabs, no buses and I had to walk ten blocks after midnight from the south side to the center city train station. On top of that, I must have been a "Bloody Mary" sight. I now know it was only the grace of God who got us all through this ordeal on that April night. When Mom came home with our new brother, she was very withdrawn. She gave his care over to me. She was not herself and I just couldn't put my finger on it, but I knew something was wrong. Later discovered, she was suffering from a condition we now call Postpartum Depression. Her experience in the whole process must have been overwhelming because there were no more pregnancies.

SERVING UP THE USUAL

There was a military family next door who loved to party as much as we did. The wife was pregnant along with me during the summer months. We sat on our adjoining front porches and drank frozen Kool-Aid for refreshing comfort. Our baby boys were born two weeks apart. Now, the partying was on for real and we called our neighbor's place, Club 100. Everyone liked to hang out there and some Philly relatives came around which made it a good time for all. Money began to get scarce. I found myself a job thinking I could move out quickly and get my own place. I saw Deon off and on after the birth of our son, Deon, Jr. He would make visits and contribute to the children's support sparingly. We tried to get our relationship back on course but somehow we never made it work. Just wasn't meant to be I suppose. Although I wanted to move out, it didn't happen right away. All monies were allocated for the upkeep of our home. Mom went back to selling booze and food at the house even though we lived across the street from a club. Our business picked up after hours and Sundays. **When times get hard, we have a tendency to revert back**

to what we know. That's how I got caught up with the married man; he was a regular at our after-hour parties.

I didn't like living home much because Mom took all the money. By Monday, I didn't even have enough for lunch. It was a good thing I could walk to work. My life continued to play out a series of bad relationships one after another. Along with working, partying and raising my kids and siblings—sending them off to school and taking on more responsibility for their welfare. At times this was extremely difficult because one of my younger brothers was getting into trouble at school quite frequently. This was likely due to a lack of male authority. His behavior continued in a downward spiral until he was sent to reform school. There were no other problems with the other siblings.

After learning my stepfather was due to return home from Nam, I was already in the process of looking for my own place. Growing tired of being browbeat if I did bring a halfway decent man home, it would only foster more embarrassment and humiliation with mom's condemnatory speeches—speeches about being unwed and having children with no father. Good advice, yes, but a tad-bit too late if you were to ask me. Although, her words and perception affected me negatively, being that I had little self-esteem and inadequate life skills from the onset. When I lost my job and found out about welfare, I signed up for a check, cashed it, moved out and became the expected statistic for that day. First in the family to become a welfare recipient and regrettably not the last, this was a decision that started a downward cycle in our way of thinking. Among all of my families' faults, laziness was not one of them. We either worked, hustled or both to make ends meet. I learned about "the system" from a neighborhood girl who happened to ask me had I received my check? I replied, "What check?" Hey, at the time it seemed to be the best way out for me to have my own place with a steady monthly income. We moved into a small, one bedroom apartment on the second floor in the city and used earthy orange crates for furniture. I took an old tabletop from the back yard and placed cinder blocks under it and was happy to be in my new Flintstones home!

After I settled into my new space, my brother Joe B. returned in my life and oh Happy Day! Although he still wasn't too happy about the direction my life had taken. He had come to visit me at least twice before. Before daybreak one morning, my mother rudely awakened me by pounding and screaming at the door. She announced that there was a call from the Philadelphia Police Department to come and identify a body at the morgue they believed to be her son and my beloved brother. I left the kids with my neighbor and went to Philadelphia on a mission that I don't ever want to be on again. Arriving at the murder scene in front of the house where Joe B. had been staying with his current girlfriend. Blood pooled in large clots on the ground where he bled to death from internal wounds. Police slowly came to the scene according to witnesses. His lady friend, we only met a few times and didn't know her very well. Joe B. had a string of lady friends after his wife's premature death. As she proceeded to tell the events leading up to him being shot, it was a night of hell-on-earth that I'll never forget. Joe B. was involved in a produce business operating out of the back of his truck with two other friends, who were also brothers. Joe B. was always a free spirit and not able to function well with inside work. An argument erupted between the three resulting in Joe B. knocking out one of the brothers outside the house. In retaliation, anger led him to go get his brother to even the score. Joe B.'s lady friend pleaded with him not to return back outside. But male ego and emotions were high enough to make him throw caution to the wind. Returning to the battlefield to face his foes and expecting a fair fight; he was ruthlessly sprayed with bullets to his chest and upper torso. He fell to the ground and choked on his own blood.

Leaving the scene, we headed to the morgue. If you never had to identify a loved one's body, you can't possibly understand the degree of grief and disbelief. Mother was suffering with a slight heart condition at the time, so it was decided it would be too risky for her to identify the body. Guess who was selected? I cannot express what it was like to see my beloved big brother. My childhood hero lying there on a gurney as if he was asleep and how I wish it was all a dream. Oh the pain, grief, sorrow and disbelief! How was I to go back through those swinging doors and tell my mother that yes, it's your first born child who was slaughtered in the street like a dog. I'll never forget the tears streaking down her face. Her eyes connecting with mine in a desperate plea to confirm it wasn't him lying on that cold slab. She was clutching my arm and interrogating me repeatedly on whether it was really Joe B.

The next time she beheld her son was lying in a coffin at his funeral in Philadelphia where he was also buried. Our family repast was at our old house where Aunt Lisa still lived. The word spread like a raging fire about my brother's death. Relatives and neighborhood folks we hadn't seen in years showed up. Such as my son's father, James McNeil, who showed up drunk and made an utter fool of himself. Constantly apologizing for his callous behavior years ago and trying to give me his wedding band. Persuading me it was rightfully mine, not my best friends, who he married after she became pregnant. Oh, by the way, she happened to be a *high-yellow gal* so his Mom approved

Too little, too late for my heart was off limits and ears were on mute. I hadn't seen or heard from him in years and I probably wouldn't have been witnessing him in a drunken stupor if it hadn't been for the family's repast.

TONIC, TOXIC AND TOILET DRAMA

Arriving back in New Jersey, we tried to resume where life left off. The aftermath of Joe B.'s death had a ripple effect that lasted for two decades, as I would find myself still crying and grieving over my big brother. Even now, some forty years later, I well up if I dwell on the horrific memories. No one has ever loved, cared and protected me like him. After receiving news that an arrest was made and trial was pending, we witnessed what was worst than a monkey trial. The criminals' mother attempted to "plea bargain" outside of the courtroom to not testify against her sons. I responded with how could she have the audacity to even approach my mother to make such a request. I exercised a little liberty and a lot of justice, in no uncertain terms, telling her where she could go! If her sons received jail time, at least she could still see them. On the other hand, my mother would never see her son again. I watched courtroom deals being made on that day *(which I was later told was with my brother's money.)* The perpetrators' mother didn't need to worry because no one was allowed to testify, only the physical evidence made the grand courtroom introduction. Staring at plastic bags containing Joe B.'s clothes, the defense and prosecutor worked on a plea agreement. Consequently, the triggerman had a heavier record of violence than his brother so they swapped alibis to receive lesser time for the crimes committed. Law-enforcement and the judicial system were at its' worse on behalf of my family. I left the courtroom more dejected and hurt than ever before adding to the pile of rejection and robbery—a stigma I became quite accustomed to.

My life continued to manifest mistake after mistake. Earl and I were in a relationship and cohabiting in my tiny apartment. We met in a nearby town in an open-air park near nightclubs and outdoor BBQ pits. Anybody who thought they were *somebody* hung out here, especially the Philly crowd. Actually, I loved the place, it had been in existence for years and even my folks hung out here. We hooked up and found out we lived a couple of blocks from one another in Somerville. The chemistry of "click" was immediate and he was exciting. Also, he didn't seem to mind that I bore four kids. Another bonus—his mother liked me too! From the onset, he treated me like a lady. I was nicely shaped with body dimensions of 34-24-38. Yes, I was "Brick House

Becky" and still attractive to behold in spite of having four children. Within a short time, I soon realized that it wasn't me he wanted especially after the way he began to treat or more accurately, mistreat me. The real motive was that I had an apartment, steady income and was willing to "give up the goods." Today, there are men who still prey on women with low self-esteem, who feel unloved or are single with children. So they can provide for him three hots (*meals*) and a cot. Meanwhile, his contributions were very limited. Yes, it was quite popular in those days to get a woman on welfare especially if you were the kind of dude that would rather lay around, sexually satisfy your woman, eat up her kids food and find every excuse under the sun not to keep steady employment. Folks, hindsight is always 20/20.

To my indignity, this was whom I selected for a husband and father of my present and future children. **When you don't know how to identify a real man or real love, you easily but swiftly end up on a path of disdain and abuse. (Hosea 4:6)** I was never skilled or schooled in choosing a man or husband. What I observed from my mother's relationships was distorted and falsified. Her husband was only home long enough to make babies, and gone off on military tours for years. They were a couple that was always happy to see each other and pleasantly in love without all the arguments. If cuss words did spew, they would come from my mother who had a sharp tongue. I inherited this, too, but thankfully God has tempered the tempest **(Proverbs 18:21).** My stepfather would simply walk out of the room and if necessary, the house. He never struck her or showed any visible signs of anger. However, while out on his "cool down" walks, we would catch the wrath of her anger. We were smart and learned to run and hide out of her sight.

When Earl and I married, I was expecting a happy, lovey-dovey, kissing, good time. Not! First of all, I accepted the first man who asked to marry me in years. With all the baggage that came with me alone, I figured I was getting a pretty good bargain. This was my opportunity to be validated and made legitimate after years of scraping the bottom of life's lonely barrel. Wow—a man who wanted to marry me with all these kids by different men. You would think after my mother made me feel like a low-life she would've been happy about my *legal* marriage. Not! Anyhow, marriage started as a "monkey show" and ended up being a brawling sideshow. Our wedding day was a comedy act, literally. We were supposed to have a small ceremony at the preacher's home. Well, lo and behold, the entire neighborhood was suddenly included on the invitation list. The poor, little preacher became flustered and overwhelmed by the growing crowd trying to squeeze into his efficient home. When we were finally settled for the ceremony, the strangest thing occurred. As I stood erect taking my vows, I had an uncontrollable urge to burst out laughing as though this wasn't actually taking place. Somehow, I managed to maintain my composure. Believe me, I should've continued laughing and walking…straight ahead and out the door!

Blowing the horn through the streets blasting our blissful announcement, we arrived at my mother's for our highly anticipated reception. Pending disaster ahead—since our wedding day fell on the same day as my younger sister's birthday. Apparently, she was upset that we stole her thunder and took the liberty to cut *our* wedding cake, serving it to any and everybody who showed up at the door! By the time my husband's side of the family showed up all the food was gone. People were getting drunk and becoming pestilent. Even my mother had a run-in with an ex-boyfriend who showed up intoxicated, feeling slighted because he wasn't the groom. Attempting to drive his car, which she didn't know how to operate, Mom mowed down a tree in front of the house! My stepfather became so enraged until he threatened to leave her. Therefore, I had to leave unhappy guests who I was trying to appease due to the lack of refreshments, and talk to him like I never had before or since. After all the commotion settled down and I finally found a ray of hope of having a "Let's Get It On" honeymoon night, my new groom was passed out drunk. Eventually, I was able to *drag him* back to my little apartment where we'd been living for quite some time. I never experienced a "wonderful wedding night" or marriage for that matter. The marriage to Earl was a big mistake from the beginning. Although the three girls that came from our union are true gifts. With all the warning signs of abuse, seems as if I would've had sense to take a quick—exit stage left. **One thing about succumbing to abuse, when you don't know how to fight, never had to fight, or stand up for yourself—you justify that you deserve what's happening to you.** My justification was who will want anyone with a sin-laded past and ugly history?

Spending a few years being a victim, my biggest culprit was identified as FEAR. After being slapped off steps, pushed down, punched, choked, held from second-story windows, threatened at gunpoint and forced to play Russian roulette.

You partner with FEAR to build a personal maximum-security prison as you learn to cope with your new norm and reality. Until this time, the only whipping I'd got was from my parents. Your psyche is enormously affected giving birth to a love-hate relationship. Sexual relations were enjoyed only if there were reasonable lapses in between abuses. I lived in constant fear of him going off at any time for no apparent reason, especially when drinking. No matter how many times "it" happens or apologies were given, I was expected to forgive, forget and be ready to submit yourself all over again.

Speaking of all over again, the babies kept coming. We were still on welfare, food stamps and lived in substandard housing. Earl couldn't keep a job because his anger spilled over into the work force as well. There was a time when we had to vacate our unit and move in with friends because our dining room ceiling collapsed on the table while sitting there. The landlord forced us to move out rather than fix the problem. I found a place on the next block over—six kids and two adults in one bedroom living in someone else's house was a bit much. But I had a good ole' monthly check rolling in like clockwork and Earl didn't have too much motivation to keep a job. Hey, as long as he held on to the kids, and me, his basic essentials were guaranteed.

After the move, this started the decline of our marriage. The verbal and physical abuse grew worse and began to affect the children. Imagine when hearing your his footsteps, it caused your stomach to knot up like pretzels. Knowing those shuffling sounds signaled either he was drunk or high from smoking pot or popping pills. A domestic explosion was only moments away. Constantly living in a state of fear, I found out I was pregnant with my seventh child. Not good news— my birth control method obviously failed. Life was so convoluted and chaotic until I was desperately praying for a way of escape. So many indignities we suffered, no one or their children deserve that.

Earl began to have open affairs with known and unknown parties, including a blood relative which I eye-witnessed the ugly deed in Mother's bathroom! My husband was very possessive only allowing me to go to the store and prenatal clinic. **Ladies, when you have an insecure person who keeps you limited from family and friends, it's generally a red flag. Perhaps, this is a strategy that keeps you in the dark so you won't find out what he's up to.** The scene I encountered was stunning, as I never imagined they would be having sex on the toilet. This experience taught me to never say what I would do if so-and-so happened. Shocked and hurt, I couldn't muster up any audible response. Becoming weak in the knees—I shut the door and leaned against the wall to regain my composure. Maybe they froze like deer caught in headlights or continued like they were in mating season, the details I would never know. My thought was if I went downstairs to reveal the steamy discovery, all hell would break loose! Mom didn't like Earl anyway and my stepfather kept shotguns under the sofa, which he would've gladly volunteered to blow his head off. In the playground of my mind, I envisioned the family's "most shameful and scandalous" memory always connected to me because of my trifling husband. How could I explain this to the children? The world's weight was suddenly resting on my shoulders. So, what did I do? I pulled together my emotions, went downstairs and acted like nothing happened. Yes, I truly deserved an Academy Award. You see, I was obsessively concerned with pleasing Mother, suffering from *approval addiction*. I spent years trying to gain her approval. Getting pregnant out of wedlock and having three additional kids before marrying not Boaz but "Bozo." I couldn't do anything right or noble in her eyes. Therefore, I felt what I witnessed upstairs would be another reason for her to disapprove or possibly "disown" me.

ON THE HOT SEAT OF DEFEAT

Returning home deeply wounded and burdened, eventually I began to write letters to myself *(popularly known as journaling).* There was no one else to talk to about my inner turmoil, so I put my pain on paper for relief. I knew God kept my mind because between my mother and my husband pulling me in a tug of war for my affection—journaling was the perfect outlet and therapy. Many other horrific events occurred during this span of my life—too many to disclose. I just hope and pray the indignities my children may have suffered during this period have long been forgiven and forgotten. **Whatever, my brother or sister, may be keeping you bound to the past; let it go and allow God to heal you now!**

Any type of love I had for Earl began to rapidly dissipate. My heart and mind were beginning to change toward my husband and mother. The realization that neither one of them loved me for myself was more evident. They both professed love but they couldn't even bring themselves to compromise and try to get along for my sake. Witnessing the selfishness they both possessed, not realizing they were tearing me apart inside. **This is what I love about God—He loves you for you! No greater feeling to know someone loves you for yourself. Oh yes, I know what it's like to be needed but to be loved during the good, the bad and the ugly, that requires a God-kind of love.** A self-wakening began in me. I turned away from them both, as I understood it was all about them. Again, they loved me for what I was to them and not for me. Blossoming into my own person and realizing that if I didn't love me no one else would either. So I stopped trying to please either of them, which didn't make me, endearing to Mom or Earl but at this point I didn't care.

Before the baby was delivered, I made up my mind that this would be the last child I would have in life. My heart grew colder by the day towards Earl but I was still trapped in fear. No shelters were established to provide assistance for abused spouses. Police just took the male spouse around the block to cool off. The prevailing mentality was wives were your private property, so do as you please. In fact they would tell you, "Call them and when I get back I'm really going to kick you're a_ _." Clearly, a no-win situation! Prevailing abuse coupled with betrayal and fear will provoke you in numerous ways. One Thanksgiving night, I was driven to the point of wanting to commit murder, and would've if my son didn't summons help from my friends down the block.

We entertained one of his relatives and girlfriend earlier in the day. We all had been drinking and after everyone went home, except his cousin and friend. He asked if they could spend the night because it was so late. I agreed and just really wanted to call it a night after being high and tired. We both went to bed. I don't know how long I'd been asleep but apparently long enough for Earl to think I was knocked out. Suddenly I was disturbed and looked up to see him peering down the staircase. My instinct tells me to stay silent. I continued to watch as he looked back to see if I was awake. I thought if he was going to the bathroom then why not just go ahead, but instead he descends downstairs. I'm fully alert now wanting to know why he is going downstairs in his underwear with company in the house. I wait for a few minutes and slip quietly out of bed to investigate. As I look down the steps, I see his cousin standing guard at the bottom, supposedly being the lookout person. He was so engrossed with the lewd act Earl was performing on this woman until he never heard me coming. I knocked him out of the way which alerted Earl that he was caught! He jumped up with his "male member" still erect looking stupid. I was cursing at him and he went straight into denial mode—calling me a liar about what I saw. He got a thick-buckled leather belt and proceeded to beat me with it. Well, I'd taken all I was going to take. I had been pushed too far. I ran into the kitchen and found the longest butcher knife and charged after him with the intent of plunging it directly into him. Our visiting guests had long ago split, *I wonder why*. He ran upstairs and locked himself in the children's room. By now, they were all screaming and scared to death. He counted on being protected because of them, but I was so over the edge my only thought while trying to kick down the door was to nail him to it with that knife! My oldest son must have climbed out the back window to go get help. I was blocking the only exit from upstairs. When our friends arrived, the husband wrestled me to the floor while he and his wife tried to talk some sense into me. I was beyond all reasoning and all I wanted was Earl dead. Finally, I ended up drinking whiskey to calm me down. It took a full three days to regain my sanity—they cared for my children, kept me boozed and Earl off of my radar. As hatred intensified toward my husband, I pondered on the welfare of my children and the fragmented pieces of my life. **Children should never be exposed or subjected to this kind of chaotic lifestyle**. Finally able to look at Earl without wanting to eradicate him was a huge hurdle. I'd conquered fear by confronting it face-to-face. Although, I regret allowing a root of bitterness to take seat in my heart believing it also affected my unborn child. Having no money, no job, and no marketable skills, was going to be challenging in executing my grand plan to haul off and leave this man. **Young ladies: stay in school, maintain your chastity, and stay away from Mack Daddies who have the potential to thwart your destiny. Don't end up living with the "my baby daddy" syndrome (See Wells of Wisdom: For Sisters Only section and Proverbs 13:6).**

BAR ROOM BRAWLIN'

After arriving home with a brand, new baby and a generous supply of birth control pills. A new attitude was on the horizon, as I didn't feel like a victim anymore. **You'll be amazed at what can be accomplished when you stop being a victim and slave to fear.** Systematically, I assumed the role of docile and dutiful wife while working my plan. The freedom bell was ringing as I began my quest for job opportunities. I'd been out of the job market for years so the picking became limited to domestic job offerings. Within, I knew I was qualified for a bit more (**Matthew 7:7 and Luke 11:9**) and discovered a program that accepted students for enrollment in business school. Hallelujah! I jumped on the opportunity like a Wal-Mart parking space. One of the perks offered by the program included childcare payments to low-income students. I was well on my way to becoming the secretary I'd always dreamed of.

After relaying this exciting news to my husband, I wasn't shocked at his attempt to discourage me. However, I wasn't allowing any negative poison to seep its way into my "dream stream." I believe the Lord even made provision for a childcare provider for me to attend school. Attending school proved to be extremely challenging with no internal support. With expectations to have dinner prepared and on time, children cared for and house kept clean, I set my heart and mind to accomplish this goal. At the time, five of the children were in school, one in afternoon kindergarten, and one in the pre-school head start program. A typical day started at 3:00AM with five heads to comb and two boys to groom. After preparing everyone including myself, I hauled them off to Ms. Winnie, a heaven-sent angel. Walking five blocks by 6:15AM to catch a bus, class began at 7:00AM and the course ran from mid-January through June. Through pre-dawn mornings and frigid cold weather, I was determined to achieve my goal and complete my course successfully. Due to my excellent performance, I was allowed to use the last two weeks to seek employment.

Swelled with pride, I received two offers on the first day. Back at the ranch, the news was not well accepted, nor did I receive a congratulatory speech only a fresh reminder to not neglect him or his house. I ended up choosing a bank in Philadelphia because of being able to work at night. My plan was for Earl to watch our children while I worked the 5:00PM to 1:00AM shift. For protection, he was supposed to walk me home from the bus stop but for nights on end, I was left to walk alone and my children were left alone while he perused the neighborhood bars. God kept us (*Psalms 91*). During these years, I never professed to have a personal or intimate relationship with God. However, I learned to pray and I can personally attest that God hears sinner's prayers. Without question, I wouldn't have made it if the Lord hadn't been on my side. He kept my mind stable with so much turmoil within and around me.

The final surprise attack occurred one afternoon, changing our course in life. Home sick with the flu, there was a knock at the door. It was the husband of my mother's best friend. Initially, I couldn't imagine what would warrant the impromptu visit. He came with an urgent and unusual request—for my husband to leave his *"woman" (not wife)* alone. The *"woman"* just happened to be my baby sister! Apparently their "steamy affair" in my mother's bathroom continued to rise. Yes, you are reading correctly—this man was married to Mom's best friend, old enough to be her grandfather and involved in an affair as well. Hit with another ton of bricks. Ouch!

After the visit, I rose with renewed vigor like never before. Intense anger can spark a new resolve you never knew existed. I decked out in a new outfit purchased for work and sat in the bedroom waiting for Earl to enter my domain. Thankfully, he arrived before the children. I invited him to sit on the bed so we could chat and surprisingly, he complied. I proceeded to deliver the message from my afternoon visitor. Before he could reply, I stood over him with a piercing look that commanded if you move you're dead. Then I uttered these new vows, "FROM THIS DAY FORWARD YOU DO NOT HAVE A WIFE! " Instead of kissing the bride, he was saluted with hawked spit.

Tears streaming and walking aimlessly, a guy who lived across the street spotted me. He stopped and asked if I wanted a ride. After getting into his car distraught, out of concern, he wanted to know what was wrong and if I wanted to talk about it. We drove to a club in another town and I poured out my sorrow over drinks. Deeply wounded with racing thoughts of retaliation, this night I sold my soul into infidelity. One night with the King? *Well, not exactly.* An affair was born which spanned over ten years. Frank knew my history of domestic abuse and had been trying to flatter me for several months. He seized the opportunity promising better treatment that he felt I deserved.

Bold as a lion, I went back home with my man daring my husband to open his mouth in protest. By now, I become a bully to fear and desperately wanted to give Earl any excuse to retaliate so I could throw his infidelity up in his face. Revenge is nobody's friend. **Dear friends, never avenge yourselves but leave that to God. For it is written, "I will take vengeance; I will repay those who deserve it," says the Lord. (Romans 12:19)**

Continuing to work my exit strategy while seeing Frank, things came to a climax while sitting in the bar across from my mother's old house in Somerville. She had moved by now—thank goodness! Carousing and drinking with Earl's two sisters, shortly thereafter he joined us and started his usual ludicrous behavior by attacking me. His sisters encouraged me not to continue to take his junk. A fight broke out between us with him chasing me. I ended up running all the way home hoping to arrive first to gather my children and escape. He must have hitched a ride because when I arrived, he was inside with the door locked and bolted threatening to burn down the house with the children inside. All of my begging and pleading proved to be ineffective. Afraid for my children's safety, I called the police. Frantically explaining the situation at hand, they quickly dismissed the emergency to a routine case of domestic disturbance on a Friday night. After attempting to access my home—they began to soften and helped to secure my children from this maniac. Earl refused to open the door at first and when he decided to—he attacked the officers, broke loose and lunged to strike at me. Resisting all authority, he punched the brick wall outside the home warranting a call for additional backup. It ended up taking six officers to restrain and bring him down. Nothing further could be done until I formally pressed charges—the point where all hell broke loose.

Finally he was arrested and carted off to jail. Our day in court was an unforgettable event. While sitting in the courtroom we heard loud ruckus and calamity coming from the holding cells. I soon learned my husband was the ringleader of it all. Before being called to appear before the judge, I had the opportunity to answer the complaint. Earl started to scream at the judge as he lunged at me, "She told you I was crazy, I know she did!" Whether he realized it or not, he was helping me win my case without my having to utter a word. The judge ordered him to be held over for psychiatric evaluation for thirty days. This positioned me of having to undergo counseling with him. I entered counseling believing perhaps we could receive the necessary help for our marriage to be saved. How naïve was I, after answering all of the intrusive questions about our life that I would still hope things to get better. After the evaluation and counseling, the conclusion was, "He'll be fine if he takes his medicine." The operative word was "IF". **Relationships only work when both parties want them to**. Losing all hope and aspiration of any relationship with Earl, I went to purchase a trunk for his belongings. Knowing I had to act quickly while he was still on forced meds. Upon his release, I demanded that he leave.

There was instant relief from fear and day-to-day pressure stemming from an abusive marriage. Over the next several weeks, I began to devise a strategy on how to move us out of the ghetto vowing a promise made to the kids and myself. However, what I failed to consider were the kids missing their father and I'm sure in their eyes, a bad daddy was better than no daddy at all. Being weary of their unrelenting whining and complaining, I, against my better judgment allowed him to return home. Even you can guess that this decision turned out to be near tragic and fatal. The police department was always on standby. I made another vow that under no circumstances, convenient or dire, would this man ever be part of my life again. And this promise I have kept! I continued to put the broken pieces of our lives back together completing the mission of leaving old things behind and beginning with a new attitude *(II Corinthians 5:17)*.

HERE'S ONE FOR THE ROAD!

With personality and mood shifts swinging like a pendulum—people who'd known me for years could hardly believe the abrupt and radical changes. The victim mentality wasn't anywhere to be found. No more wimpy, sissy stuff. Life transformed me into a monster—yes, a lean, mean, cussing and fighting machine possessing the hardest of hearts. Frank, my lover, was still in my life, we had an on and off relationship for several months and even shacked up (*lived together outside of marriage*) for a period of time. During our brief time of co-habiting, Frank proved to be a disappointment in many areas. It's ironic how folk can make you feel like you are the cat's meow until they get you. With all of the known issues he knew I'd gone through, he repeated a lot of the same drama. We found ourselves arguing a lot about other women, which eventually led to our multiple breakups.

Still receiving aid for my children—a visit from a social worker wrote a life-changing report. He left the report visible giving me enough time to read and review it. The report contained an undeniable proposition: whether I wanted out of this house and neighborhood? After answering with a resounding yes, he began to reveal a plan by which I could start the process of purchasing a home immediately if I had fifteen dollars. Sounding too good to be true, I happened to have the money upfront. If nothing else, Frank kept me with access to money. To my amazement, the social worker guided me through the process of purchasing my first home for only fifteen dollars! And he even gave me advice on how to keep it from being claimed by my husband if he happened to show back up. After Earl left for the second and final time, he caused a great deal of problems. Apparently, he became involved in some type of trouble in his hometown and persuaded the authorities that I was mainly responsible for his behavior. He cited lies that I was a bad wife and mother so much until they started to investigate and question my neighbors concerning me. After getting wind of this, I became furious and went straight to the investigating body to clear my name. Certainly I didn't appreciate them asking my neighbors probing questions, besides, if there was something they needed to know, now was their opportunity to address me in person. What right did they have to do this? After all lies were cleared, I was happy to get over that hurdle because I refused to take off another day from my job to deal with this non-sense again. Another chapter closed and I was even closer of ridding myself of a terrible husband.

A lovely, all-brick, three bedroom single-family house with an enclosed glass porch on the best side of town became our new abode. The day we moved was sheer excitement for me. Leaving behind the naysayers as they gazed tickled me pink! Why people don't wish to see you do well or improve your life remains a mystery to me. Some even talked about the raggedy junk I left behind for trash pickup. What's even more ironic is none of these haters ever offered to help this single parent raising seven small children single-handedly. Being the second Black family on the block, we had great neighbors in our new neighborhood. Mrs. Kay and her family next door were good and healthy for us. She taught and exposed me to so much—introducing me to fine china and glassware. She eventually left me with some very, lovely pieces.

The new neighbors, who replaced Mrs. Kay's family, had kids who were close in age with my own—which made things nice. I began work for a bank in the city, which was nice and convenient because I could catch the bus on the corner from our new house. Working hours were perfect—

leaving after the kids went to school, and arriving home in the early evening. My children were old enough to stay alone for a few hours as I kept check by phone until I arrived home. Life was beginning to settle a little. Frank and I were back together as an item although his constant moving in and out made the relationship stormy. This was the classic case of a soul-tie because although I knew he wasn't good for me and not what I desired. He seemed to have this spell overshadowing me where he'd conveniently enter and exit my life causing me to terminate any other existing relationship at a moment's notice. I couldn't realize it then but now I know it was only lust that kept me strung out on him. **Remember that true, authentic <u>Love</u> gives and <u>Lust</u> takes without regard to no one but self.** During one of our "Love-Lust" periods, we seriously discussed marriage. He showed up with a ring and proposed one night. My response was "no" because his motive was impure. Deciding to propose to me after he discloses the news about some girl he got pregnant while his mom was away hospitalized. Being hurt and angry all over again, ended up throwing him and his ring out in the street.

If we would've been two sane and responsible adults, we probably could've made the relationship work. We had a lot in common especially with him working in law enforcement and I ended up working in the same field too. Our combined salaries along with child support placed us in an income bracket far above our peers during those years. Although he never was a good steward over financial resources just privileged to have the gift of prosperity but didn't know what to do with it. Case in point, when a settlement came from an accident we squandered it carelessly. Yes, I take the blame for my part in this as well. No money management skills and the lack of financial knowledge hurt us pretty badly. The best thing I did was purchased a family car and learned how to drive because he even abused this privilege, by riding other women around town advertising that it was "*his*" pretty new car. Well, I rained on his parade quickly and sent him stepping out of my life one more time.

During this timeframe, I was accepted into a lucrative law enforcement program. I'd mastered the civil service test, passing in the top one percent and was accepted in the field. I trained extremely hard and was proud of my achievement so I wasn't about to give up the best job I ever had. Although working swing shifts were no easy task, but we learned to adjust. There was a series of men I dated but never allowing any of them to move into my house. I experienced so many failed romances looking for true love. I took the reverse male approach by using them to get what I needed and then leave. This seemed satisfying for a while but ended up being pretty lonely because the reality of living with stupid and pathetic choices didn't make life easier at all. Imagine running around with a crowd that drank and partied as a hobby.

STAGGERING BUT STILL STANDING

If there was a party happening anywhere in town, you can bet your bottom dollar that I was "in the house!" People spotted my car parked at various locations and automatically knew that a party was going on or about to happen. In my world, I thought this was popular and loved every minute of it. But in hindsight, I was just another party girl blowing money on booze, perpetuating a history of poor choices. **Proverbs 20:1 states that wine produces mockers; liquor leads to brawls. Whoever is led astray by drink cannot be wise.**

Of course, men always wanted to date me because of my Coke bottle physique and flashy acumen for fashion. Nope, I never declined an open invitation to hang out in exciting places and party events around town. But in reality, my party presence became merely a trophy on display because no one *really* wanted to take me home to love, honor and cherish. This devalued mentality and way of life became a huge part of who I was. It was normal to live in a perpetual dysfunctional state. Working with mostly men in the correctional facility, became an easy access to all the brothers I needed. It afforded me to have guardian males ensuring my protection and their benefit was having a Friday night girl to make sandwiches for their card games. It was clearly communicated and accepted by their wives and girlfriends that nothing frolicsome was going on. My relationship with the guys and their families and friends was extremely healthy and trusting. I mostly kept my dating relationships outside the department. *I feel your co-workers shouldn't be privy to certain information that you deem confidential.* Contrary to popular opinion, I'm an extremely private person. You may ask, why are you disclosing so much "private" stuff throughout this book? As you continue to read, you will soon discover why.

My children were growing up so fast and I was feeling the sting of single parenting. My older children left to stay with their dad(s) figuring this would provide a greater sense of balance and settlement for them. During my marriage to Earl, they had no example of a proper father figure. Between him going into a jealous rage when one of the kid's dads would come to visit finding any opportunity to create more havoc in the house, it caused more emotional and psychological damage giving them more reason to move out into a more stable environment.

My excessive partying didn't cease either. I met Randolph who I regret until the day I take my last breath. Based on the series of events that occurred, he must have been watching me. We got caught up in a whirlwind romance where I knew someone was wholly interested in loving and cherishing my children and me. He invited me home to meet his mother and family—they had a very lucrative business. We wined and dined with the best. **There must have been plenty of red flags, but when the devil wants to deceive you; you are a willing participant (James 1:13-15).** Thinking I had everything under control couldn't be further from the truth. I discovered, after agreeing to marry him, that he was a cocaine dealer. My life was suddenly turned upside down again. I took a leave of absence from my job and sent my two older girls with him to Texas and kept the two younger ones with me. In the meanwhile, I still needed to settle affairs back home. Talk about a ludicrous move! God was with my children watching over and protecting them because upon my arrival in Texas, they were well and reported nothing happened during my absence. Randolph secured an apartment just as he promised. It was fully furnished with everything setup for us, and the following week we were on schedule to be wed. When we went to get blood work and obtain our marriage license, the place was closed. It was a holiday weekend and I completely paid no attention to the day. I was so focused on finally settling down into a real family situation. I guess you could say, I was stuck on stupid and glued on dumb.

The plot was beginning to unravel because within a few weeks, Randolph was becoming more aggressive in personality. He was often on edge and paranoid. His supply of cocaine had been depleted and his plans were in disarray. He wasn't working, food was running low and the rental furniture was due for another payment. He publicly announced we had to move because the rent hadn't been paid. This was very disturbing news because the girls were already in school and I assumed we would be stationery for quite some time. We didn't ever end up getting married, which turned out to be the best course of action anyway.

Why Randolph insisted on us moving to Texas was beyond me. We moved in with one of his uncles, who welcomed us reluctantly. He treated us nice but there was always a vibe that he wasn't too thrilled to have the "clan" to move in. After realizing I made a tragic mistake by moving, I tried to make the best of an unfortunate situation for our family. The proverbial straw that broke the camel's back was when Randolph and I were in a grocery store. He attempted to force me to steal meat. And after I refused, he slapped me so hard until I saw stars…and stripes. I broke down in tears, which immediately drew attention in the public place. Abruptly, I was grabbed by the arm and led out like a prisoner of war hauled away against my will. Fear resurfaced again and took on the personality of panic this time. **Psalms 34:6 states, this poor man cried, and the LORD heard him, and saved him out of all his troubles.** Consequently, Randolph got locked up. His uncle conveyed the news along with the advice of not getting involved with his no-good nephew. He continued to state that I seemed like a nice woman, so the best thing for my kids and me is to flee and stay clear of him.

I heeded his advice and didn't waste any more time. I called back home to ask my stepfather to come pick us up. Thank God, he did, rescuing me from another bad choice once again! He wasn't feeling well but arrived on the same day backed up a U-haul, loaded it and we all left for New Jersey. Good-bye Texas. Ironically, he never questioned what went wrong, lectured me on my stupidity or reprimanded me for my foolish decisions. He simply came to my rescue for which I'm eternally grateful. Our drive back home was quite precarious. He must have over compensated a turn because the truck's trailer went one way and we found ourselves hanging over a cliff! Fortunately, he was able to navigate the truck and trailer back into alignment to continue our journey in safety. ***Psalm 91:11 states, "For he shall give his angels charge over thee, to keep thee in all thy ways. "***

ANOTHER GOOD TIMES RERUN

Arriving back home in New Jersey, I found my house in shambles. I allowed my sister and her kids to occupy the house moving in from across the street. The plan was for her to eventually take over the mortgage. Her current landlord was collecting rent but not paying the note on the duplex where she lived in. The plan was perfect so I assumed her family could have a nice home while my credit stays in tack. It came to my knowledge that the furnace malfunctioned, filling the house with smoke and unsafe levels of carbon monoxide. This was the root cause for them moving out and rightly so. The home, however, went unsecured, as I was never advised of the faulty furnace or the abrupt vacancy. Thieves broke in and ravaged my home, taking various household items as they ransacked the house. Adding insult to injury, she never paid the mortgage either. So my return home was welcomed with drama at the front door. Not placing blame on any one else but myself because it was my house and therefore my responsibility.

I was blessed to have a job to return to. Tried settling back into the routine of mother and provider for my children but the daunting task was more difficult than ever because a history of poor stewardship caused me to fall behind in my bills and financial obligations. On top of that, I couldn't afford the furnace heater repairs and the walls of foreclosure began to shadow box me in. Trying to play catch up on your finances seems like a losing game in itself. Falling further behind every month, dealing with late fees, collection calls and notices; you feel as though you are drowning in a sea of debt!

One morning there was a knock at my door. Upon answering, there stood three women: Randolph's mother and two of her friends. She began yelling for leaving her son in Texas and not informing her that he was in jail. I explained that her son was incarcerated because of his own misdeeds and criminal behavior. My children and I were fortunate to get back home safely. Besides after the way he treated me, I didn't owe him or her anything nor did I want any contact with him whatsoever. One of her tag-a-long friends was a well-known radio personality. It would've been a pleasure to meet her under different circumstances. The ladies continued to bring all types of threats and accusations against me. At this point, I realized communicating on an intelligent level was not effective. The only way I could get them to vacate the premises and stop these embarrassing and humiliating accusations was to zip up my "gorilla suit" and go ballistic on them! Yep, that worked. I never heard from them again. His mom thought if she showed up with a well-known person of influence, I would be somehow intimidated. What she didn't consider was I was mad with the "entire" world and wasn't taking anything that remotely resembled nonsense from anyone! They really picked the wrong day and time to mess with me. *Parked on Anger Avenue is where many of us find ourselves after having messed up over and over again. Our anger spews like poison on everything around us when it's really ourselves we are mad with! We really have to begin to grow up and admit when we blow it. The process is to repent, turn away from error, stand corrected, do the right thing and continue to move on (II Chronicles 7:14). Don't stay angry, throw a big old pity party and look for everyone else to resolve your problems. Surely you*

will reap what you sow and it's vitally important to sow good seed in good soil (Galatians 5:7& 8).

I lost the fight and had to move out of my blessing into another home on the other side of town. A friend's friend had a house she was willing to rent with a lease option to buy. My children left their friends and familiar surroundings taking a tremendous toll on them. During this time, my four eldest children left home and were off doing their own thing. I was a grandmother for my oldest daughter had a baby, and my oldest son was about to welcome his first child. No one was married and history did repeat itself. Started to experience mischievous behavior from my children in school—they began to act out and their school grades began to slip. I was forced to intervene and stop them from hanging out with a certain crowd of young girls, who had a track record of shop lifting from local stores. I may have been a lot of things but a never a thief and wasn't about to have my girls lead a life of crime.

Seems I was an easy target when my daughter, Darlene, asked to spend the day with a friend in our old neighborhood. On the way to work one morning, I dropped her off at the friend's house and agreed to pick her up after work. She apparently had other plans including spending some quality time with a former neighbor's son. Her plot of deception worked until the wage of her sin was revealed when she found herself 5 months pregnant. Only thirteen years old, I plummeted into a deep depression. I contacted the fourteen year olds' parents and made them aware of the situation. Hoping we could get together and make the best of the situation, the day of the Terry's visit turned into a terrible experience. Mrs. Terry did most of the talking by stating there would be no help coming from them. If this really was their son's child, he was too young to support it and they certainly were not going to provide support. You know the old adage…Momma's baby and Daddy's maybe. Mr. Terry stood there as if he wanted to say something but couldn't muster the courage to spew it out. Once again, I saw my past staring me right back in my face with a gruesome snicker. See, I assisted my oldest daughter through her pregnancy until she finished high school. Although her choice, her boyfriend did want to marry her. Now I'm faced with a new dilemma, another daughter being cast with a generational curse. I rose up out of ashes of depression and confronted the fact that I'd been making some pretty silly decisions in my personal life justifying them by putting the blame on family issues.

In response to the Terry family, I saw red! I ended up putting them out swearing and declaring in that in no uncertain terms, whether they helped my daughter or not, the grandchild would be taken care of. I had no other choice because she was too young to take care of herself and he was too young to take to court even if I wanted to! My daughter learned a valuable life-lesson that day in a way I never wanted her to experience. From that moment on, I devised a care plan for her and the expected baby.

It was an icy, cold January day when baby Kia arrived. Seems like we slid all the way to the hospital because Darlene was ready to deliver! She was rushed straight through to the birthing chamber with nurses in tow. I was told I must go through the proper channels but there was little time for delays, the baby was ready to enter the world now. We came to the hospital earlier but the visit was deemed false labor. This time there was no mistake about the timing of the birth. I waited with great anticipation for my new grandchild to "meet and greet" the world. The doctor had little to do when he finally arrived. Perhaps I paid him for nothing since I did most of his job! ☺ Thank God, the delivery was successful and we brought new mom and child home. I fell in love with our new addition. Only the best was good enough for her. Yes, I began to spoil her…most Grandmothers do☺. My daughter and I had a serious talk about how this was not going to happen again especially without marriage and a husband. She made me a promise it wouldn't and I made her a counter-promise that if this wasn't the case, I wouldn't be available to help. Glad to report that we both kept our promises.

A few years thereafter, I was able to give her a wedding and send her off to start a military family life with her husband. As Darlene was leaving, I allowed my oldest son and girlfriend move in—they were expecting and since I was ready to leave this house, I let them move in believing they would do the right thing. Yep, sounds like another episode of Good Times, eh? But they weren't responsible and I was at risk of being in trouble with the landlord, facing possible jail time or losing my job *(hadn't a co-worker intervened on my behalf).* Thankfully, all turned all well. Hopefully, I learned my lesson for doing good deeds for family.

LOOKING FOR LOVE

The girl's lives turned out to be ok after all. They ended up living with their Dad for a while. I started to believe the lie that perhaps I wasn't capable of doing a good job raising them and since their Dad remarried, life may be better for them. Besides I had been threatening to send them to their father if they didn't straighten up and behave. In reality, I was being selfish and wanted to be free and have the right to explore my freedom, without the weight and responsibility of raising children. I wanted to live for a change! My self-gratification cost my girls dearly because their Dad didn't treat them well at all. Today, thank God, they are grown and self-sufficient women. I earnestly believed that God has healed all wounds and scars that occurred through improper choices.

Distressing news came that my baby girl became pregnant. She was another young teen mother operating under the generational curse. **How to rescue my family out of this gridlock of whoredom and** *unwed motherhood—a bondage embedded deeply into the family's bloodline? Now I know, but didn't then, that it would be only through the saving grace of Jesus Christ! These cycles become a normal part of life if no one ever stands up, fights and confronts it.*

My girls knew when they left, they could always return home. Of course, neither took me up on the offer. Could you blame them after feeling unwanted and unloved? They remained with their Dad until they were able to go out on their own. Perhaps this was one of the reasons, my baby girl got involved with a much older man. She began her quest of looking for love and not knowing where to find it. What better incentive for them to leave and make the best of their own lives? Clearly, we parents had no understanding or wisdom in proper child rearing **(Proverbs 22:6).**

Though my youngest daughter had a son, the father didn't end up marrying her. We all thought she was going to lock up with the love she was longing for. Her older sister, Jean, came to the rescue by finishing high school and moved into a place where they all could live together. They made life work against all odds. Today, they are wonderful mothers in their own right. Jean married, divorced, became a homeowner, became born again (*saved*), and is currently raising two Christian college students. She accomplished this through much sickness, pain and the turmoil of crippling arthritis, which eventually confined her to a wheelchair. None of these enemies stopped her from serving God, and raising her two children in the Lord. She was the typical soccer mom riding around town to all of their sports events. She even maintained stable employment during these peak periods. The fruit of her labor were children who were super proficient in their respective sports—winning and placing first on national levels. My youngest daughter owns her home and is an astute businesswoman, having owned and operated a daycare service. **In spite of all my shortcomings in their upbringing, God has been faithful to answer my prayers by blessing their lives and their children's. Most importantly, they still love and respect me as a mother, and a woman of God.**

My seasons began to shift as a new single woman in a new apartment for the first time in my life. I was presently in a dating relationship but the relationship wasn't valid. He was married and having big problems at home. Neither of us thought things would become as serious as it did. We met at my favorite neighborhood bar and spent as much time as possible because we hung out with the same crowds in the same places. As anyone could imagine, I was so fed up with unfruitful relationships until I wouldn't settle long enough to hear any fellow's rap or game. I dressed sharp and looked good at all times—hey, finally living out my dream at least so I thought! I wasn't lacking in male companionship and besides I had all my fellow shift officers to hang out with anytime I wanted. So I could afford to toy and play men just like they did women. Hey, I had nothing to lose and I could care less. Slowly past hurts and disappointments crept in and began to consume my heart again. Layers and layers of hurt and pain still existed that never have been penetrated. When Ed and I began to talk it was because someone else stood me up. He actually knew the guy and felt honored to take me out in his stead. By now, I'd downed a few drinks and said what the heck! The truth was I really didn't know too much about him except he was in our in-crowd and always alone. So we went on our first date. We were very compatible friends before we became lovers. Isn't this how most affairs start out, someone who's compatible and takes time to listen? We'd talk for hours. I became acquainted with and knew all about his martial woes, family, job, and social issues. It seemed that someone was finally interested in me for a change, and not just looking for an affair. Calling a spade a spade, that's exactly what it was though. Somewhere along the line it became much more than that. I started to care about this guy, much more than I should. Not wanting to be branded a home wrecker again, I encouraged him to see if he could remedy things at home between him and his wife. If nothing else I've learned that wives always won…*right or wrong!* In addition, I was preserving my emotions figuring I could exit gracefully before plunging in too deep.

On the job having daily contact with the inmates, who were infected with everything under the sun **(Romans 6:23),** I contracted a viral hepatitis. I couldn't believe the company doctor's report, so I went to my personal physician who not only confirmed the diagnosis but also sent me directly to the hospital from his office.

With off and on nagging symptoms, I knew something wasn't quite right with my body but I conveniently ignored them. Although I had plenty of experience with drug users and knew about hepatitis, I'd never been close enough to be aware of the symptoms. Assuming one could only get it from drug addicts sharing dirty needles *(Hosea 4:6),* I soon learned you could become contaminated from several ways. It's highly contagious through food, water, and sex among several different types. Currently, there was only Hepatitis A from food or B, which most drug users were affected by. Well, my case didn't fall into any of those categories. After repeated blood work, lying in quarantine, puking my guts up, I knew for sure I was going to die. After 30 days, it was determined I had A nor B. Since my case didn't fit in the typical category profiles, it was hard for the medical professionals to determine the root cause of my disease contraction. My physician and I determined it most likely came from a bite while assisting two inexperienced officers with restraining an inmate. **As a further testament to God's goodness, this peculiar type now known as Hepatitis C, is suppose to remain in your blood system forever. As of the writing of this book, no test has shown** *that I have any trace of Hepatitis C or any other kind! God's is good and His healing power does and will always work for his people!*

Though the event was unfortunate, I believe it worked in my favor. Perhaps it was an adversity to cause me to stop and slow my roll in life. Perhaps God allowed this—not caused but allowed it to secure my future. I have always felt He was calling me back then but I didn't recognize His voice and continued to go my own way. During those thirty days, somehow I knew this was one of life's defining moments. Because soon after being admitted, I sent for my toiletries at home and requested for my Bible. Yes, the one that was encrusted with dust and laid dormant except when accompanying me to a few church services…Christmas, Mother's Day, Easter, and New Years Eve. I began to turn on and watch all of the Christian channels on television. **This time was used to reflect over my life to seriously think about the meaning of my entire existence…**because up until this date, the notion was beyond me.

The Lord started to deal with me in my everyday affairs especially on my job. There were several groups of women from various churches who would come, bring gifts and minister to the female inmates in the jail I was assigned to. My fellow officers and I labeled them as the "goody two shoes" women. We weren't thrilled when they visited because A) it interrupted our scheduling and B) we knew most of the women were only taking advantage of their kindness. When dealing with the incarcerated, scheduling and timing is everything. Order must be maintained at all times and it's crucial to keep control of the environment. The church ladies would even witness to us officers from time to time. There was one lady in particular, who would always take the time to personally invite me to her church. I would've never thought that her husband would work with a young lady who later became my daughter in law. Anyway I promised that I would come so she could leave me alone. Ironically, my mother had a sudden notion to attend church again.

A TASTE OF GENESIS

While home alone one morning, I awakened to a Voice calling my name. First I thought it was my imagination. Turning back over to get some much-needed rest after completing a 12AM-8AM shift, again, the Voice called my name, "**REBECCA**." I was more convinced this time it must have been God calling me. But wait a minute; God doesn't talk to people *like me*. When I got up to bathe, I looked in the mirror and my mouth was slightly contorted. I kept staring at my face with disbelief trying to reconcile what could've happened. I went on to get dressed in prep for an afternoon hair appointment. Besides, I was off from work that night and needed to look my best! Taking no further thought about the condition of my mouth, my beautician immediately noticed it and commented, "Your mouth is twisted, isn't it?" Dismissing his comment altogether, I convinced myself and everybody else it was simply the way I had my moth positioned. Leaving the beauty shop, I sashayed across the street to my favorite bar, and found a party. I could still sense the climate of my life was about to change, remembering how sick I became the last time I'd taken a drink. **When I reflect back over my life, I see the handprint of God's love trying to woo me. His grace and mercy were and are still constant companions.** My mouth returned to normal, I believe I suffered a mini-stroke. **God is good!**

After being diagnosed with Hepatitis, those thirty days offered me the time to be quiet and escape from the crowd. I came to terms with my condition and began to learn as much as I could about the disease. My man really stuck by me during my illness: he paid my bills, shopped, and kept up the apartment. The illness caused him to have a sentimental connection with me. Actually, I forgot all about him being married because he was there for me day and night. Life at home grew worse for him—not condoning our affair as being right but his marriage was doomed before I stepped into the picture.

I arrived home with a new attitude without knowing I'd been changed. Returned to work and tried to pick up the fragmented pieces of my old life but it was no longer working. Old friends stayed away from me like I had the plague, not even wanting to eat the things they used to love for me to cook for them. Slowly everyone in my immediate circle backed away from me. Later I discovered, they distanced themselves because of the disease, being misinformed about it altogether. Oh well, I now realize it was God separating me from them. Now I was ready to give Ed the ultimatum of choosing between his wife and me because I knew what we were engaging in was wrong. Remember, being the other woman is just that—"*other.*" Ed's daughter became deathly ill. **Oftentimes; tragic situations bring the worst of enemies together as allies.**

Knowing what would most likely occur, I recommended he go back to his family. Remember, as I stated before, wives always have a way of winning. His daughter eventually recovered fully and things at home became problematic again because he was right back in the streets. He began to hit on other women, making me jealous and I expressed my feelings to him. I figured if he was going to be with someone, why not me? We continued where we left off with one exception—we started to live together and I wanted marriage. I told him to get a divorce, as I would no longer settle for being the other woman. My eyes were becoming open since hearing some words of wisdom along with "the change" experience. Growing anxious to listen to the church ladies witness to the female inmates, fear began to grip my soul. As I started to read their *(inmates)* Bibles, I didn't know one scripture but started in the back with the book of Revelations *(not the ideal place to start for new Christians, by the way).* By now, I was baptized and attending church regularly with my Mother. Yea, baby, we're on the right road now with this new "church" thing. We filled up an entire pew with my children, grandchildren and other friends who tagged along for the ride. There were rumors and unrest developing within the congregation about the lascivious behavior of the Pastor. However, I was admonished not to pay any attention to the allegations, and I didn't. Maybe I should've taken heed though because apparently the Pastor left in disgrace, which left two deacons one Sunday morning battling over who should take the reigns in leadership. Yes, you read correctly they were actually fist-fighting in the church pulpit! Disappointed and disgusted, I marched my pew warmers right out the door and never returned. After that incident, I literally stopped attending church. I rationalized that this was no better than what the church was calling "the world". It was the same behavior I experienced in the bars and clubs.

In the middle of the chaos, I caught my first glimpse of a strong, saved woman who loved God. I watched her every week as she sat in her seat, looking distinguished than anyone else in the building. She wasn't dressed any differently, or did anything special to cause her to stand out. It was just her confident composure and demeanor. She was the essence of virtue—the anointing of God seemed to envelope her.

Meanwhile, one of my co-workers, already in a backslidden state, started taking me to church with her. This church was one of those good, old-fashioned, sanctified, Holiness churches. Ed and I would faithfully attend with her. I fell in love with the music and the preaching was good. Hey, what did I know? As soon as we would leave church on Sunday we would all come back to my place and she and Ed would drink beer together. After a few times, I didn't want to go as much because the services seemed to go on forever. I couldn't see spending all day in church on Sundays.

My friends began to drift apart. They either wanted no part of me, were stuck in some Holiness church looking like drab old ladies or their husband's left them after some time. I came to the conclusion that there must be something wrong with this church stuff. To top it off, one of my daughter's started to go to church and started talking to me about how a woman is suppose to submit to her husband. I told her she must be crazy because wasn't no man gonna rule over me—her father was already enough. The behavior I observed from her "so-called saved in laws" on her wedding day didn't help her case any. The preacher and father-in-law, turned out to be a bad apple with his wife leaving him because of his prevailing issues. **As Christians, we must never become stumbling blocks, see I John 2:9. In all this I know God was still showing me grace and mercy because of the seeds being sown and the watering was well on the way.**

Ed had made up his mind and the divorce was almost final. Some delay came after his wife realized he really wanted a divorce. She devised a plan as a last ditch effect to put her marriage back together, that plan included a sudden spurt of religion in hopes for reconciliation. Since someone else wanted him, he became desirable again. By this time his son was living with us and I was making arrangements for college money. I was not going any deeper without a firm commitment of marriage. On Christmas, he officially proposed to me and we were engaged. My ring was pretty and unique—it was my birthstone, Garnet with diamonds. I was a happy camper for about a minute. **Happiness typically depends on "what's happening". Joy, on the other hand, is not based on circumstances, but it comes from within (Nehemiah 8:10.)**

One night, Ed's son woke up complaining of stomach pains. Assuming it was an upset stomach, I suggested he take an antacid and go back to bed. By morning, his condition grew worse and he called his mother, who was a registered nurse by the way. She transported him to the hospital; apparently he suffered an acute appendix attack. After being released, he returned home with his mother. As for me, I was relieved from the burden of raising another teenager, especially because he was giving me a lot of trouble lately. ***It's true, in most cases that children emulate the behavior exhibited before them***. He saw firsthand his dad and I who were living together, drinking, and partying—so he felt he had the right to follow suit regardless of our opinions. Coming home to find him drinking "our booze" with friends and his girlfriend in "our bed" wasn't going to fly. His untimely departure was a welcomed relief.

DON'T CALL A CAB, CALL A LIMO!

At work one day, I was skimming through a real estate book, and came across a house that I absolutely fell in love with. I remember thinking if this house has everything this profile states—I'm going for the gusto! Three- bedroom, ranch style, stucco home sitting on a beautifully landscaped three-quarter acres in an upper middle class subdivision. Rushing home like a little kid with a new toy to show Ed our newfound dream, we agreed to make an appointment to see the property. We also arranged to view a few upscale condo homes while in route. The agent never showed up. While waiting, we met a resident who tried to sell us on the place by telling us that sports celebrities lived here. We weren't impressed but was highly ticked off that the agent stood us up. We translated the "no show" to we're not wanted here. Continuing to our original destination, when I set my eyes on the house, I knew it was a winner! We were in awe taking the first tour through what was to become our new home. The interior matched with what we already owned. The price was right and all the options and perks were in our favor. Life was coming together for me finally. I left believing possibilities were at our fingertips.

Ed left wondering where we were going to get the money. I had a good job and good credit and besides, I borrowed money to send his son to a school he never attended-which I paid back already, so why not borrow money for my dream house? I started the paper work right away. In the meanwhile, a fellow officer was selling raffle tickets for an all expense trip to the Bahamas, my favorite vacation spot on the planet. I bought two and we won the raffle. It was November and a perfect time to escape the cold. This opportunity became our honeymoon. We were already engaged and planning a July wedding for the following year. This was Ed's first time and my second trip to the islands. A friend gave us a limo ride to the airport, which was another dream come true. It's a privilege to ride in a limo while upright and awake, not lying in a coffin. Wonderful times we shared in the islands, with friends already there, we had more bang for our bucks. After the trip, we began to finalize our home buying plans and move. Financing was cleared and by Christmas, we were all set. Since we were to settle around Christmas, we opted to let our seller stay over the holidays since she had all of her decorations displayed and all. She didn't expect her home would sell so quickly. The transition worked out well for both parties. Super Bowl week of 1984, which just happened to coincide with my birthday, we moved from the city to our first subdivision. Ed borrowed his company's truck—my son and his friends helped with the move. Wow, we finally hit it big time for not many of "us" lived in professional subdivisions. One huge celebration took place...a combination of the Super Bowl, my birthday and the new move. In hindsight, it was truly a victory that I give credit to the Lord for. After arranging the last decoration, the place looked as if we lived there for years. Now we needed to get used to the twenty-five mile commute back and forth to the city for work; but It didn't bother me in the least because for the first time in my life, I experienced a real sense of accomplishment. I had a brand new home, a husband *(well almost)* a good job, my health, money in the bank, excellent credit, fine clothing, jewelry, and a loving family living the ultimate American dream.

Two months later, I pulled into the garage and opened the mudroom door; I knew something was terribly wrong. Our little Cockapoo met me with bathroom tissue entwined all around him. As I looked around the kitchen, I knew our house had been burglarized. Not knowing if the intruders were still on the premises or not, I grabbed a butcher knife as I approached the phone to call the police and carefully began to go through the rest of the house informing the intruders I called for back up and would use the weapon at my disposal if necessary. Thankfully, they had left the scene but every room of our house was vandalized. The heavy, custom-built front door was open and locks were broken, apparently, these thugs used planned and concentrated effort. When police arrived, I already begun to canvass the house to access the damage not wanting to touch or displace anything until they thoroughly reviewed the crime scene and dust for prints to see what was missing. After closer inspection by us, we realized the person(s) were looking for something specific. No usual household items were missing. All drawers, closets, cabinets, shelves, boxes, and containers were opened and ransacked indicting they knew what they were looking for. After a final analysis, nothing turned up missing except a ring and pair of cuff links belonging to Ed. It was determined that during their quest, they were stolen because they liked the items. It clearly wasn't the focal point of the robbery from the damages incurred to the durable front door. Their motives just didn't make sense. Ironically, the body powder container was emptied all over my bed so we assumed they came looking for drugs. This conclusion brought back to memory that shortly after we moved in, the former residents' son shown up one day and asked if he could go into the garage and retrieve something he left. What an unusual request for a clean, wide-open garage with no items visible. However, I told him he was welcome to look if it would make him feel better. Besides, I had no reason to suspect him or his mother of any illegal activity. We recently completed an extremely lucrative home and furniture deal together and everything seemed legit. He retrieved a small package from the rafters, thanked me and left. I mentioned this to Ed and soon forgot about the incident until now after the home invasion. Now, I consider this as another hidden blessing from God because things could've been adversely different for us had we been home when the intruders came for what they believed to be on our premises. The stolen items were never recovered but did receive some sort of justice in that the perpetrators were brought up on other charges. I picked up the 4-1-1 from my inside contacts within the law enforcement system.

After this episode, we settled into a nice, quiet life—the life I dreamed about for so long. This season was truly the happiest of my adult life. Slowly but surely, the happy moments began to unravel, not certain how or when but when your foundation is not grounded and rooted in the principles of God, life will crumble like a flaky, piecrust.   After several months in our new home, I had a dream:

> ***I was standing in a field with a wooden slated fence on my left. I could see a male friend of mine who had recently died sitting on it swinging his legs back and forth. To my right, was his wife who remained alive. This couple was friends of Ed and I; we partied and drank together all the time. Directly in front of me was Ed, and directly behind him was a light…not just any light but the brightest light I ever beheld in my life. As if under hypnosis, I walked away from everyone straight***

into this "light." Unsure how long I stayed in the "light" but when I returned everyone was in the same place as before. What has happened to me? All I could sense was that I was different. I looked directly at Ed and exclaimed with a resounding voice: "IT'S TRUE, IT'S TRUE, HE HAS COME BACK!"

Ed gazed in amazement, pushing past me slightly, and said "LET ME GO SEE FOR MYSELF." He went into the "light" and when he reappeared, he looked differently too! His countenance changed just as mine did during my experience. Not aware at the time but now I know that the infinite God gave me a glimpse into my future! Some twenty-five years later, I'm glad to report that yes, I walked into that marvelous "Light" of Christ. The man on the fence was already deceased; his wife, we eventually lost contact. And Ed, we're still waiting on the manifestation.

This dream troubled my soul greatly. I began to inquire to those who professed salvation in hopes to gain a deeper sense of meaning and spiritual perspective. An officer buddy suggested that I start to read the Bible. I took her advice and it was the beginning of a newly found adventure for Becky Birch! Like a nerve-wrecked novice, I stumbled upon the book of Matthew, chapter 28, verses 1-8; this passage of scripture seemed to connect instantly with my spirit. Although I had no real understanding, it was like having a sixth sense that I was on to something beyond my deepest consciousness. As we continue on with our lives, I archived this experience in the back of my mind. One night, I remember being home alone with the sudden urge to kneel and pray. This was an event that I hadn't actively participated in years; therefore it was no surprise when I couldn't recall a single word. Though I was taught the Lord's Prayer just like so American children, what one doesn't use, one will surely lose. My spiritual reality check was humiliating but apparently not enough to open my Bible to re-acquaint myself though.

BARSTOOL TRANSFORMATION

With summer was fast approaching, July was in clear view and I was busy carrying out wedding plans. One afternoon on the way home from shopping, I stopped by one of the taverns I used to frequent, and host occasional dinner parties on the weekends. Being well known by the staff, I wanted to chitchat with one of my barmaid friends. Truthfully I missed the camaraderie and atmosphere. The early evening crowd was light as they listened to jukebox music engaging in lively conversation. As I sat on the barstool, my attention was drawn away to a large picture window on my left. When I turned back suddenly everything and everybody in the place was nerve racking and annoying. The music was too loud, the people looked silly, and I became agitated thinking that all of this is really getting on my nerves! I shook myself and attempted to enjoy my time out. But the longer I sat there, the more aggravated I became. Next time I spoke out loud, "This music and noise is getting on my nerves." An internal voice spoke, ***"NOTHING IN HERE IS ANY DIFFERENT THAN IT'S EVER BEEN, AND IF IT'S GETTING ON YOUR***

NERVES SO BADLY, WHY ARE YOU STILL SITTING HERE?" WOW! I immediately asked my friend if I owed any tab for my soft drink I'd been sipping. She replied no, and asked was I leaving already? **YES, IT'S TIME FOR ME TO GET UP OUTTA HERE!** This was the last of my bar room days. Yes, the omnipresent God showed up at a bar and transformed me sitting on a barstool, *thus the title of this book!*

Meanwhile, the prison ministry volunteers were serving dutifully and bringing gifts of mercy every week. The lady who always prayed for me continued her plea about visiting her church. The following week, my friend *(who I was currently going to church with)* asked me to attend a revival. I agreed to go and felt impressed to extend the offer to my mother to accompany me. We weren't on the best of speaking terms, not even exchanging a simple hello for months. Miraculously, she agreed to go. After work, I commuted twenty-five miles to get dressed, as if I was embarking on an important date *(well, I most definitely was!)* My hair was a creative piece of art. My interior was graced with the choicest of undergarments. My exterior was cloaked in a fine two-piece suit. Along with new hosiery, matching

131

heels, and elegantly scented perfume. Tonight was MY night! I drove another twenty-five miles to pick up Mom. As soon as she was situated in the car, I apologized to her and asked for forgiveness for our petty disagreement. It really should've been the other way around, but at this point it didn't matter who was right or wrong. Besides, my mother wasn't frequently known to apologize to my siblings or me—that was a no-no according to her worldview.

Our long twenty-five mile ride back to the city was peaceful and harmonious. When we arrived, the saints were praying and praise-and-worship soon followed. A lively saint, on the row behind us, was beating a tambourine like a stepchild in my mother's ear. I was a little apprehensive knowing she wasn't used to these kinds of services. Thinking any minute she might be ready to leave—another miracle she stayed. During testimony service *(dedicated to hear personal accounts of what God has done for others.)*, someone began to speak in tongues *(heavenly or spiritual language)*. My friend leaned over and whispered if this really were of God, someone would interpret the tongues. Then an old church mother stood up and prophesied that the speaker was a true man sent from God with a message. Needless to say, all of this was intriguing. I'd heard of "tongues" before but hey, I didn't believe in any of that stuff. For sure I knew Mom was ready to leave by now, but she just sat still in quiet observance. The guest speaker was a male evangelist from California and I can't recall his message that night. However, the altar call was tailored just for me. The call was specifically for healing of the body. For some time, I'd been having sporadic chest pains. I went up thinking I would be prayed for but soon as I approached him, he asked what he could he pray for me. In the middle of my reply, he quickly asked if I had been baptized. "Yes, in the Name of the Father, Son, and Holy Ghost." Don't ask me why I answered in that manner for at the time I didn't know there was a difference. He then asked, "Why don't you get saved, God is trying to save you tonight." This was the most profound night of my life. I began to weep and sob from deep within like never before. I began to cry aloud, "I'm so tired" over and over again. My hands went straight up and I felt as though I was being lifted up into the air. If I yielded, I would've gone straight up. I could hear the people in the background lifting up praises to God. The guest minister motioned for the mothers to come forth to take me back to be baptized. What was all the excitement about? Hey, I didn't want to go with these people. I was shaking my head in absolute denial, but all I could utter was, "I'm so tired." Subconsciously I was thinking what on earth is wrong with me? I'm living my best life and have everything I desire—a beautifully, landscaped ranch styled home with in-ground pool, fancy clothes, good job, restored health, and stable finances. Icing on the cake—I was about to be married to a man that I love with all my heart.

Busted! I was under Holy Ghost arrest. Yes, the big bad Sheriff's Officer with handcuffs and gun was now under a different kind of authority and power. I was led away stuttering and muttering, still shaking my head in protest not able to speak a word. I was helpless and needed to be undressed and placed in a white robe to prepare for baptism. This is why I believe I had a sudden desire to dress in my best *(inside and out)* because I had a divine date with the King of Kings and Lord of Lords! Who, by the way, is a merciful

Gentleman, and doesn't ever make you feel ashamed. God knew I would be surrendering my life to Him in an Apostolic Holiness Church among strangers whose practice was to immediately dunk you in the water. **Now let me clarify that, I don't preach for or against what name you are baptized in, just do it for the Bible commands it.** But I believe, this night was ordained that I be baptized in Jesus name as it states in **Acts 2:38** and my life has never been the same. I sobbed the entire time I was being dressed for baptism. I didn't stop until I came up out of that cold water. The same sister who ministered to the female inmates, prayed for me, and invited me to church, got to see the fruit of her labor. She was one of the women who dressed me, and her husband took me down under. The seed was planted, watered, but God gave the increase *(I Corinthians 3:6)*.

After witnessing my conversion, my mother stated she hoped I'd enjoyed this church better than my last experience *(implying her church—the one I left a few months prior.)* You can't tell me God doesn't have a sense of humor. He showed up and showed off on that night. Ironically, I had a head on collision in front of this same church on a Mother's Day morning coming off the midnight shift. I walked away without a scratch! It was as if God said, "The same spot you *(the devil)* tried to take her life is where I'll save her." I returned home that night in awe still not fully comprehending all that took place. I informed Ed of tonight's event and he didn't seem too impressed. I can honestly say I didn't *feel* any differently but my life began to change right away or I changed rather. The first noticeable change was I stopped cursing. Oh, I used to curse like a sailor. I discovered this when I visited a church closer to my home. I wanted to worship closer to home because winter was approaching soon. Apparently, the Pastor knew about my recent experience, so when he looked at me that Sunday morning and said, "I've been waiting on you. " I looked at him like he was crazy. His next sentence really floored me, "God has sanctified your tongue." It was at that moment when I realized I'd not cursed in weeks. I shouted and asked the church to pray that I receive the gift of the Holy Ghost. When I made this request, I didn't even know whom the Holy Ghost was. Well, I wouldn't have to wait long as I started attending this church right after that Word of

Knowledge was given to me. In a Wednesday night prayer meeting, I was on my knees trying to pray but my mind was beginning to stray. I began to refocus in prayer when I felt my legs being lifted up. I looked around to see what was happening but nothing. Dismissing it as my imagination, the same experience happened with my hands. Again, I looked around to see, nothing. Now, I was convinced that I'm totally losing it. Suddenly, I was on the floor, rolled under a pew and landed on my back. I never stood upright that night. It was as if someone or something flipped me over. I don't know how long I was in this state, but I do recall the Pastor leaving the pulpit area and anointing my head and hands with oil. When I tried to stand up—helpers arrived because I was drunk on new wine *(Holy Spirit)*. With assistance, I was able to sit in a pew. No sooner than I sat down, I jumped to my feet, hands lifted, and filled with the Spirit of God with the evidence of speaking in unknown tongues. Thanks unto God; I'm still speaking fluently today. I left church in a state of euphoria, mesmerized by my new experience. I called my naysayer friend who told me I'd never receive the Holy Ghost while living with Ed but while talking to her, I began to speak in tongues! She was hosting a prayer meeting at her home when I broke the news and they all rejoiced and began to speak in their heavenly language. God is awesome and He doesn't need anybody's opinion to do what He wants whenever He wants to. **Now let me clear up any notion that God honors sin in case you are living with someone and assuming God doesn't mind. The devil is a liar, always was and forever will be.**

There was a separation between Ed and me after that night. We still slept in the same bed but it was as if we were total strangers. I was clueless to the ways of God till I couldn't fully appreciate what was happening. I was sanctified *(set apart)* and didn't even know it. Ed and I hadn't been intimate in weeks and I wanted to know what was wrong. When I tried to be intimate, Ed's response was strange. He had no interest and stated it was like I was his sister. Wow, look at God! **He stepped right in the middle of my mess and started cleaning me up.** As I look back on this season of my life, I do believe it was the beginning to an end for Ed and me. Even though we did get married, things were never the same after I got saved. We were unequally yoked but I didn't know that then ***(II Corinthians 6:14).*** We proceeded with our wedding plans and I won't elaborate on the details other than to say, God granted my heart's desire.

SHAKEN, NOT STIRRED

I was stricken ill two weeks before the wedding and ended up in the hospital. It looked as though we would have to cancel for sure. However, four days before, I managed to pull it all together. My youngest sister had been staying at my house during my hospitalization *(volunteering to help run my house in my absence.)* Big mistake! When I returned home, my home environment and atmosphere changed. Ed didn't seem happy to see me home when he arrived from work. I wanted to surprise him but instead, I got surprised because of his coldness and nonchalance. I began to set my house in order by sending my sister packing. During her short visit, she developed a takeover spirit, and I wasn't about to be second fiddle in my own house.

Finalizing wedding plans, I made calls to vendors, friends, and confirmed RSVP guests. Touched base with the bridal party, ordered the cake, and told the caterer *(my best friend)* that the wedding was still on!

On the wedding day, it started to rain—a sure sign of a pending disaster since this was an outdoor event. Folks were saying that I couldn't set up a tent and chairs around my pool in the rain. Well I did. At two o'clock on a beautiful, sunny Saturday afternoon in July, my marital status changed. Thanks unto God because even my children were thinking Mama was crazy. I told them God promised me a rainbow and there can't be one without the sunshine and the rain! My wedding theme was, *The Rainbow* and a rainbow wedding we had. God smiled upon me one more time. Our reception was less than desirable though. There were a few folks who used our occasion to disgrace themselves and used the time spent at our event as an alibi. Again, I didn't experience a honeymoon night *(eventually I'll have one, you think?☺)*

Ed and I began to drift more and more apart. To him, I was no longer his beautiful party girl—drinking, smoking and dancing the night away. As I grew closer to the King of Kings, he grew closer to the "lord of liquor and king of beer." His excessive drinking became a big issue in our household and marriage. I fussed and complained—he listened but didn't stop. The inevitable happened—staying and straying away into the wee hours of the morning and eventually MIA *(missing in action)* for days on end. I was getting used to being in the beautiful house alone. My house was not a home. As I look back, I didn't handle marriage well because I lacked wisdom. **And believe me, it takes God's wisdom to adjust to the early years of marriage, not to mention one between saved and unsaved partners.** My ex-husband was a good man who just could never accept being loved. His idea of love was always performance-based. He thought material things equated to love. This was his mentality, he didn't know any other way. As for me, all I wanted was to be loved for who I was. I guess he just didn't get it. I know what it feels like to be needed, that's all I've ever been was "meet" to someone else's need. Therefore being loved for who you are remains a <u>*biggy*</u> on my list of values. I assumed he would have wanted the same. We struggled for four years trying to make things work out. There were more ups than downs. Spiritually, I was growing by leaps and bounds but I was a public success and private mess.

Ed would no longer go to church with me so that's where I resorted to spending the majority of my time, while he was in the bars drinking. God was manifesting Himself more and more. I tried to win Ed, but I probably made all the mistakes that the majority of unequally yoked couples make. Things would've definitely been differently twenty years ago had I Godly wisdom. Again, hindsight is always 20/20 right?

The Call on my life came amidst of a messed up marriage. There was such a hunger and thirst for God, his Son Jesus, and the Word of God. It was like sweet candy and I savored every bite. Yes, I was still on the planet, but everything seemed different now. I was beginning to sense things I never knew existed. My current level of fellowship was no longer satisfying my hunger. I thirsted and desired for more, wanting to be taught more than the preaching *(hollering and screaming)* I was currently receiving. I sought out School of Ministry and was blessed to find an opening right in my neighborhood. I learned more about the Word of God and even the professor recognized the calling on my life. This was discussed with my current

Pastor, which he made a public declaration. I was promised acceptance, and ordination; however, this never took place under his leadership. I remained faithful and continued to serve—being happy to be saved alone. When the professor asked had I been ordained, he was surprised that I hadn't and vowed to take care of the matter when the next graduation and ordination services were scheduled. I loved school and have always loved to learn. This was special though because I was learning on a whole new realm and dimension. At work, things were changing for me also, as folks were beginning to notice "the change" in me. So much until my born-again experience was being tried and tested on a daily basis. That's the reality of having a reputation, good or bad, people expect you to live up to it. No longer was I the cussing, drinking, and smoking Becky they were accustomed to.

Now, I had weekends off—a promotion I'd been seeking for years. I was transferred to the new facility with an office, desk and phone. I believe the Lord reserved this for me because He knew my past desire was to party all weekend but to serve Him only now. I shared a washroom with three other male officers; it became a place where I developed a prayer life. I scrubbed it thoroughly everyday for I was before the throne three times a day praying not to mess up. I won't lie and say it was easy because there were plenty of times I had to reach out and call prayer warriors to pray me through. Don't exactly remember when the shift came where respect replaced reproach among my fellow officers. All I knew was suddenly the atmosphere changed but God received the glory from my changed life. My transformation was so radical and complete—my co-workers knew it had to be a Power beyond their capacity to comprehend. **It's a miracle when God steps into your life and makes you a new creature in the midst of those you've known for many years.** Especially when you left one way and returned completely different the next day.

I never failed to witness to my co-workers about what God was doing in my life. For instance, on my way to work one winter morning, I turned onto the freeway with hardly any traffic. How unusual because it was morning rush hour. It snowed a few days earlier and ice and snow were still visible. There was a car ahead of me and another car two lanes over. Suddenly, the car across from me collapsed like a horse when it breaks its' front leg. The entire wheel detached and came straight toward my windshield. I screamed JESUS! It sailed in the air landing on the roadside. I never lost control of the car but was pretty shook up. After arriving to work, I must have looked and sounded like a mad woman recounting the wild adventure of my morning commute. I know now it was one of my guardian angels that swatted the wheelbase *(with tire attached)* as I called on my Savior. I had been praying for increased faith but not since have I prayed "that prayer" as I needed no further affirmation on increased faith.

THE "OLIVE" MAKES THE DIFFERENCE

My ordination took place in Philadelphia. There was a massive crowd while many were graduating, being consecrated, receiving degrees, and special honors. Several of my classmates along with myself were blessed to be in that number. As we walked across the stage on Saturday morning, more than forty well-known, distinguished men and women of God laid hands on us and declared our callings. Oh happy day, finally, an accomplishment that someone could be proud of! Ed and a female minister/friend *(who later I served under as an assistant pastor)* attended. Both congratulated me but if only Ed had put his arms around me and said, "Honey, I'm so proud of you," would've meant the world to me. But that fairytale ending didn't happen—no one even took a picture. I masked my disappointment because over time, that's what you learn to do.

The need for increased ministry became apparent so I started giving clothes and food away out of the back of my car. Whatever I could do to spread the love of God to those less fortunate than myself, I did. I started helping a sister clean the church, then served in the tape ministry, and later became head of the usher board. Whatever I could do to serve, I was willing. I tried to get my husband involved in what I was doing, but wasn't successful. Recognizing the need for advice, I sought counsel from church leaders. It didn't help much in those days especially being in a hard-line Apostolic Pentecostal fellowship. The real truth is Ed wanted no part of the church or I because he felt the church had stolen his girl. We became two people who occupied the same space at certain times, but our marriage was going…going…gone! To relieve my misery, like many other women, I buried myself in church, school, and work. Matters grew worse at work too because I became disobedient ignoring my call for full-time ministry. I kept reminding God that I'm losing my husband already, we have a new home, bills need to be paid and my salary is the highest. We needed the money so my husband would never go for this…*yada, yada, yada.* Meanwhile, things were so crazy at work. In over twelve years of service, suddenly there were no uniforms in the whole department to fit me. My stuff was getting really raggedy by the days, scheduling was crazy; judges were getting upset with me. I thought I was in a mad house half the time. I'd rehearse on the way home how I would break the news to my husband. My granddaughter *(my first convert)* would sometimes ride in the back of the car. She spent the weekends with me. Between her own tears, she would ask what was wrong with me. I'd, in turn, ask if she was ok. Finally figuring out, the Spirit of God was moving on her and me as we rode down the road every weekend. On one Sunday morning, my granddaughter walked down the aisle and gave her life to Christ. I was overjoyed. Shortly thereafter, she received the gift of the Holy Ghost with the evidence of speaking in tongues. Actually, as the Lord blessed her, several other children were touched by God's love as well.

As a last ditch effort to avoid full-time ministry, I made a deal with God that if my husband didn't agree, then I couldn't either because I'd be disobedient to him. We know how to give ourselves wiggle room, don't we? Knowing Ed would never allow this, I finally spoke to him about it. I rehearsed what I was going to say over and over again. Heart pounding, I ended up blurting it out all at once. He just looked at me and walked away.

I thought, "Oh boy, I'm in for it now." Within 15 minutes, he returned to the room and told me to do what I had to. Now what? No more excuses. Forced to make a decision—either plunge into faith or dive into continued disobedience unto God. Foregoing the latter, I wrote a letter of resignation and started out on a journey that I assumed to be paths of peaches and cream. Wrong, wrong, wrong! I wouldn't classify my choosing to resign either good or bad but the reality didn't match my expectations. For starters, I had no proper guidance or training, but God always bless those with an honest and sincere heart.

The more Ed stayed out all night, the more I'd stay awake worrying and praying. Eventually, I stopped worrying and continued to pray. His drinking escalated as our household affairs continued to spiral out of control. I returned to work in the nursing field this time. Hoping the increased and steady funds would make a difference. I ended up getting fired for the first time in my life. Left with limited choices, I tried to reason with Ed by requesting that he go his way and I go mine, and we sell the house before we lose it. We were getting close to the edge. He expressed he didn't want to break up; realizing things would have to change for us to stay afloat. Nothing changed. We became so far behind until it seemed almost impossible to catch up. God had been faithful—promising me He would make up the difference concerning our finances and He did just that. My husband was blessed with a promotion with a substantial raise. ***It's never God's fault when our lives turn awry, oftentimes we are our own worst enemies.***

OLD WINE, NEW WINESKINS

Eventually, we lost everything, which was the worst day of my life. Imagine being put out of your dream home by the Sheriff's Department you were once an employee of. It's the epitome of ultimate humiliation. For the first time I looked at my husband with disdain as the movers packed our personals. Gazing at some of his masonry signs, I thought, Ed really believes that junk is going to save us when he chose to ignore all sound legal counsel and Godly direction. Oh, what a crushing experience as I stood on the sidewalk and watched my door being padlocked, water turned off, and furniture hauled off to storage. I packed as much clothing as our two cars could hold including books and Bibles. We drove around for hours. **Women, nothing is more devastating than to follow a man with no plan, no direction and no vision.** As nightfall approached, I was tired of going *nowhere* so I asked to be taken to my brother's house.

When we arrived, I assumed he would request to temporarily stay until we got on our feet. Not! I humbled myself, made them aware of our situation and made the request on his behalf. My brother was shocked to learn of my present fate. Traditionally, I was the tenacious one that helped everyone else. Thankfully, he opened his door so we'd have a place to rest our heads. Soon thereafter, the state of affairs in his house became equally dysfunctional, making it miserable to inhabit. My plan was to be "gone" as soon as possible and Ed was in agreement. I was always unsure of what kind of effect this really had on him as a man. I could never get him to express his true feelings, which was one of the main problems in our marriage—lack of communication. What was so weird was when we were dating and living out of wedlock, we talked all the time. I can't even remember what we talked about but communication was at an all-time high between us. **The "silent factor" in any relationship is deadly because it leaves too much speculation as to what the other person is really thinking.**

I received plenty of promises of finding a new home but the reality was a husband who was in a drunken stupor nightly. I'm quite sure our present situation was devastating to him and his self-esteem as well. Trying to be patient and allowing him take the lead; time proved that it just wasn't in him to think beyond himself. ***Sadly, when a man has no one to teach him or example before him how to be a man, he most likely ends up fumbling his way through life doing the best he can. Hoping everything will miraculously turn out ok.*** Ed was a good man with wonderful traits, but like me, no one taught us what life and love was all about. This explains why we got along so much better before my spiritual regeneration. I experienced the Light of God's love and grace while he was still in darkness and wanted to remain there. Our living situation was getting critical with mounting pressure from my sister-in law concerning Ed coming in drunk and falling asleep with lit cigarettes that burned their furniture. One morning, I gave him an ultimatum, either the booze or me. He chose the booze and I chose the door!

I Ended up renting a room from a friend's friend on the Jersey shore, where I also landed a job and was able to save enough money for a condo. Stopped by the storage unit to claim our belongings and not to my surprise, I didn't have access. Ed and I agreed to meet so I could gain entry and while there, I extended to him a place to live where he was welcomed at any time. His response was, "I'll think about it. " I removed some of his furnishings and clothing items but he never came. I held on to his clothing as I hoped we would have an opportunity to reconcile at some point. You see, I was still holding on to that dream of him "walking into the light." **God can give you a promise concerning someone else but He will never violate anyone's will. In other words, if a person is unwilling to receive what God has to offer, it is ultimately their loss. God is not a man who will lie neither is He capable of lying. (Numbers 23:19)**

Eventually, I learned to move on without Ed. I became ill again and my children moved me back to the Somerville area. My personal belongings went back into storage. I was supposed to stay with my eldest son and his wife, but ended up at my mothers instead, the last place I wanted to be! However, while there I learned why God allowed it. I discovered some undesirable family traits that needed to be dealt with personally. **There is no room in the kingdom for ungodly behavior that goes on without being checked.** Being sick and without income, I learned humility, patience, and long suffering through sorrow. A real low point was receiving public assistance—assistance that made a reservation in my name at the Welfare Motel. Moving into these three rooms was a nightmare, wrestling with roaches every night for weeks. The Lord blessed there though, the bugs left my area and none came nigh my dwelling *(Psalms 91:1-7).* Though this seemed like the lowest point, it was really where I developed hind's feet for high places *(Psalms 18:33).* My faith for healing increased as I had time to spend alone with God meditating day and night on His Word. I lived to go to church and my spiritual hunger and thirst increased on a daily basis. **Pain, sorrow, and suffering will increase your capacity of compassion. You begin to look at life with a completely different perspective.**

For some financial relief, my disability insurance payments finally came through. Upon leaving the motel, the manager commented that he never had a neater and cleaner person who resided there. Glory to God! I witnessed to him how I was able to survive for the past few months and leave with boxes stacked from floor to ceiling because God's increase met me there. I secured an apartment and retrieved my belongings from storage. It felt mighty good to have my own place again. There were so many ups and downs during this season as my faith was tested greatly along with sudden declining health. For the next three years, I was in and out of hospitals. My liver condition deteriorated from chronic hepatitis to cirrhosis, right up to final stage for liver disease. Literally, I was on my way out of here. Swollen like a full-termed pregnant woman with puss oozing out of my toes. This was my "Job-etta" experience and like Job, my critics murmured that I must have sinned for this tragedy to befall me. I learned to pray for them while walking through this valley of the shadow of death. **God was faithful during this extreme time of testing. In one of my most painful moments, He gently whispered in my ear, "My grace is sufficient for thee. This sickness**

is not unto death. You shall live and not die and declare the works of the Lord (2 Corinthians 12:9-10, John 11:4, Psalms 118:17.) Glory, hallelujah, He always keeps His Word. The physicians in NJ suggested a liver transplant was my only hope and they wanted me to go to Pittsburgh. This was out of the question because I didn't have the means for a transplant in PA nor the family networking for program approval *(an important part of the process.)*

While in remission, I allowed my son and his family to come stay with me, much to my regret. We moved to a larger apartment to accommodate his family. This, too, didn't work out well. Between trying to finish college *(I had received free tuition),* studying, and helping with the grandchildren, problems began to arise. I was no longer willing to tolerate the living conditions as I found myself wanting to inflict bodily harm to my own son. Two of my daughters moved to Virginia, and got wind of what was happening. They moved me to Virginia. For the "nth" time, my belongings were shipped off to storage again. After arriving to VA, I detested the place and after my granddaughter's graduation, I planned to move back to NJ. Not realizing that the Lord had other plans for my life. ***Many are the plans in a man's heart but the Lord's counsel will prevail (Proverbs 19:21).*** Shortly afterwards, my daughter moved to a neighboring city in VA. I resolved after helping her move, I was leaving. A few weeks later, received a phone call from the storage manager back in NJ, informing me a check I sent for payment bounced. I was appalled as there was no rhyme or reason of why the check returned. I investigated what was going on. She informed me that the check specified to see the "Maker", a banking term I was totally unfamiliar with. Investigating further, I told her I would send cash to redeem my check. I went to an A T M machine to get the cash. When I inserted my card, all kinds of bells and alarms went off signaling the card was fraudulent. The bank had been notified of my death and froze all of my assets. When I spoke to my bank, they interrogated me thinking I was pulling a scam. After investigation, we discovered at a funeral home in Philadelphia, a body with a toe tag identified as being me. Imagine almost being arrested for impersonating yourself! Apparently, no family member was informed of my "untimely" death. I was dead and didn't even know it

159

(perhaps I forgot to lie down. ☺*)* Now my plans to flee VA came to a screeching halt. Where can one go with no money? It was several months before I was able to work with Social Security to straighten this mess out. My original caseworker underwent surgery in the middle of the process, which delayed things even longer. Alas! One day I stopped in to check on the status of my case. The receptionist recognized me and said, "Let me check the system to see if you have been resurrected." At that divine moment, those words became crystal clear and sealed my fate. It was orchestrated by the Lord to keep me in Virginia, a sent place where I would begin a new life. God knew I would never leave New Jersey voluntarily. The events that followed proved my word of knowledge to be true. By the time my case was resolved and back on track, I landed a job and settled in with my daughter. Even though, my health at the time was not good, I was taking pain meds in order to work. Later I learned that the kind of meds I was on wasn't good for my present condition. It was toxic for my body and contributing to the swelling.

TAB—PICKED UP AND PAID IN FULL!

Living with my daughter was not working out well either so I applied for an apartment. Denied on the first attempt, I needed a cosigner. Surely, no one was going to do this for me, I thought. I took this matter to the Lord in prayer. One morning as I drove to work, a "Now Renting" sign seemed to jump out at me. I figured it was a sign from the Lord and promised to stop by on the way home. When I did that afternoon, I received a second rejection. Well, I prayed again. This time I was directed to bring certain paper work when re-applying. I did just that and received a phone call that I could move in right away with a discounted pro-rate. Yes, God is good! With no furniture or basic necessities, I was so happy to move into my one-bedroom place. Nothing else mattered at that point. God continued to prove Himself faithful. Friends began to donate the essentials and oh, what a blessing! Shortly after moving in, I became too ill to work. The job lasted long enough to qualify *(on paper)* for my place. Glory to God—He knows how to come through when you need Him most.

My oldest daughter who had nursing experience became concerned that my current physician wasn't the best for me. We visited one of her colleagues who had the expertise that was required. My first consultation revealed my present state—only three months left to live. The good news was if he could keep me alive long enough to receive a successful liver transplant, I would have a good chance of living a normal life span. His plan didn't involve my going to Pittsburgh either. He had friends who were participating in a new program in a neighboring town approximately fifteen miles from where we were staying. He promised to do his best to get me accepted in the program. This surgery would cost thousands of dollars, which I had zero of those dollars. My doctor kept his word and I was accepted into the program. Hallelujah! **God knows just where you ought to be to receive what you need.** My mind reflected on the circumstances that led me to VA, my initial unwillingness to stay and all the fuss and stink I made about being here.

My case was graciously accepted and I began preparation to be treated for the transplant. My new doc began treatments for me to become well enough to withstand the transplant. It was not easy. There were days I crawled like a baby, unable to stand until the swelling went down. I survived numerous hospital stays, losing great amounts of blood and causing me to have seven (7) surgeries before transplantation. During one surgery, I had a strange encounter with death. There was an adverse reaction and infection in my gall bladder. The pain was so intense. I thought childbirth was the ultimate pain but this was ten times worse! Thank goodness I was already in the hospital when the infection developed. From early that morning, I sensed something strange and different. Couldn't really describe it but knew this wouldn't be an ordinary day. While being transported, lying on the gurney and looking up at bright lights in the ceiling, I sensed that this time I wouldn't be coming out alive. As the anesthesiologist administered, I whispered, "I commit my mind, body, soul and spirit to you Lord." My last conscience memory was a voice saying, "YOU CAN'T HAVE HER, SHE DOESN'T BELONG TO YOU!" Days later, I awoke in a cold, dark room.

During surgery, I stopped breathing and was put on a respirator. With no memory of when or how I arrived here, I was totally immobile and hooked to up to wires and tubes everywhere. A nurse's aide, who had befriended me and was also saved, slipped into the room to check on me. She told me she had been praying for me and wasn't supposed to be on my floor. However, she wanted to see if I had come around yet, since the doctors thought I had a very slim chance of recovery. She knew the Lord was with me and that I would wake up. She also informed me that my daughter gave her strict instructions not to tell me I had stopped breathing and was put on a respirator. I told her it was ok and that the Spirit of the Lord already revealed to me that He kept his Word and rebuked death for my sake.

Now, I was in a healthy enough state to start the transplant program. I was placed in intense therapy to see if I was mentally as well as physically able to endure the process. I had to establish my family network and support structure, receive all kinds of shots, and walk daily to build lung capacity. I will always be forever grateful to my oldest daughter, Dee and her husband, who hung in there with me during this process. Her willingness to take me to endless appointments, along with coaching, and encouragement when I wanted to give up will never be forgotten. She was there holding my hand the night when the call came all the way up to the surgery suite. It was as if I was looking at a movie of someone else as I lied there looking at yet another anesthesiologist preparing to sedate me. Indeed, this was super-serious—this time operating on the arteries. He numbed both of my wrists, cutting them open to thread. I was told I had to remain awake during this part of the procedure so I wouldn't bleed to death. Imagine watching someone slit your wrists and sew them back up *(thank God for Jesus!)* I was told the operation took over six hours to perform. After awakening, I was in excruciating pain. My briefing on what to expect post-surgery didn't compare to the reality of what I was feeling at the moment. Immediately, I knew something was wrong. The inability to move my legs and abdominal pain were too much to bear. I tried to signal that something was terribly wrong but the doctors/nurses assumed it was just a natural reaction. There were tubes in my throat and in every other bodily orifice, making it nearly impossible to communicate. Finally able to get the attention of my daughter to hand me pen and paper. My message was passed on to the proper Doc for my issue to be addressed. They discovered I had a major, internal hematoma *(localized swelling filled with blood resulting from a break in a blood vessel.)* Immediately, I had to go right back to surgery! Ouch! Ouch! Ouch!

Within three weeks, I recovered well and was at home learning how to adjust to a brand, new life. Several months later, I received an invitation to meet with my donor's mother. The invitation stated there was an agency that worked with organ donor families and recipients who wanted to connect. This was done only by mutual agreement and I was elated to know this lady wanted to meet me. She accepted and RSVP'd for dinner at my home. When she came to the door, my heart started to pound. Previously, we exchanged letters so we knew some things about each other. However, meeting face-to-face was another matter. She was a very pleasant, kind, and forgiving woman. Holding her eighteen-month old granddaughter in her lap, I sat and listened as she talked about the tragedy that befell her daughter that night and how she made a decision to donate her daughter's organs. This woman's daughter (*Caucasian*) was married to a Black man. Unbeknownst to the mother, he had been an abusive spouse to her daughter. Her ultimate escape from the abuse sent him into a murderous rage that led him to not only shooting her, but also her friends who came to the house with her to retrieve her child's car seat. She made an immediate decision at the hospital to donate her daughter's eyes, heart, lungs, kidneys, and liver, which I received. There had been no prior commitment or arrangement for this gift of life. Of all the recipients, I was the only one she requested to meet. What makes this so unique is, I too, was a victim of spousal abuse. Let's look at picture, this woman was white, I'm black, the man who killed her daughter was black, and she wanted me to know that she was glad the recipient was African-American. In addition, she wanted her granddaughter to know me when she was old enough because she still shared her with the other grandmother, which she held no animosity. She wanted her granddaughter to know her African American heritage. What an amazing woman and she wasn't even saved! **God was showing me where I was coming up short in mercy, grace and forgiveness.**

What a humbling day for me. I received another miracle from this woman. I witnessed forgiveness in its purest form. Her daughter's best friend came along to visit and seemed to miss her friend dearly. After the dinner, we continued to keep in contact until I was impressed in my spirit that our communicating was causing pressure within her marriage. Apparently, her spouse wasn't as forgiving as she was and I confirmed this with her later. She went back to school and was teaching classes and giving lectures on abuse. I have been free of disease for more than twelve years and counting! **God truly makes all things beautiful in its time! (Ecclesiastes 3:11)**

Jesus Christ has picked up and paid our "eternal tab" and destiny is calling us to deeper wells, wider territories and higher places in Him!

TO GOD BE THE GLORY!

A PSALM OF COMFORT
Psalms 40 (Verses 1-5)

I waited patiently for the Lord; and he inclined unto me, and heard my cry.

He brought me up also out of a horrible pit, out of the miry clay, and set my feet upon a rock, and established my goings.

And he hath put a new song in my mouth, even praise unto our God: many shall see it, and fear, and shall trust in the Lord.

Blessed is that man that maketh the Lord his trust, and respecteth not the proud, nor such as turn aside to lies.

Many, O LORD my God, are thy wonderful works, which thou hast done, and thy thoughts, which are to us-ward; they cannot be reckoned up in order unto thee: if I would declare and speak of them, they are more than can be numbered.

Wells of Wisdom

People our lives are like ripples in a pond. When one throws a rock or stone into a body of water, it causes a ripple effect. Every life decision or choice we make will affect the sphere (or spheres) of influence we are connected to. Our lives are not about us. We need to be careful of what we do as it is often said, "Someone is always watching!" We were all born with a God-given purpose. However, it's up to us to hear His voice as He draws us with His bands of love. It's up to us to accept Jesus Christ as our personal Savior. For Christ truly died for all of our sins—so receive the converting of our souls as He desires for all of us to do.

~ ~ ~ ~ ~ ~ ~ ~ ~ ~

Within these pages, I have opened up and shared through the history of my life in how God was

dealing with and drawing me to him with His love, patience, mercy, and grace. He stepped out of eternity and into time right in the middle of my mess! While sitting on a barstool, He opened my eyes and transformed me from a clueless young woman to a child of salvation through grace. My desire was to give a glimpse of unnecessary consequences when we live contrary to God's Word and instruction for living. His laws and precepts are sure; so take heed and learn to listen and obey. So subsequent generations and we won't suffer the consequences of wrong choices and actions. Don't set in motion, generational curses by not adhering to His word. Let's benefit and reap the reward of blessings, and not curses (possibly taking years to eradicate or even generations to come.)

Let me provide some Biblical examples of a few principles discussed earlier. Let us begin with Adam and Eve (Genesis, Chapter 3). We all know that their choice to eat the forbidden (fruit) caused mankind to be born in sin and iniquity. Their firstborn son Cain, murdered his brother Abel (Genesis, Chapter 4). Noah decided to drink a little too much and ended up cursing one of his sons. Abram and Sarai foolishly decided to circumvent God's will and promise and set in motion two nations who are still at war today. Continuing in the book of Genesis, Jacob always gets a bad rep for being tagged as a trickster (con artist). By the way, I'm a champion of the underdog so to his defense, I researched and discovered what preachers usually don't preach about concerning Jacob. If you research his family tree, you will find that his Momma (Rebekah) was raised in a house with a less than honorable man, Laban. So when the opportunity arose to deceive her husband, her son (Jacob) whom she thought should get the Patriarchal Blessing was instructed to carry out this deception, even though he protested (Genesis, Chapter 27). This was her norm within her sphere of influence. She became a product of her environment and what she emulated was embedded in her. As you can see, she encouraged her son Jacob to do the same. This caused a ripple (cause and effect) in the family, creating instant hatred between brothers. Laban also deceived Jacob fueling a dysfunctional family, and love triangle between sisters, which continued throughout generations. The moral—bad choices can create generational curses.

David's sin with Bathsheba brought adversity and death within his own household (II Samuel 12: 1-25). Now, let's go to New Testament scripture. The handpicked twelve disciples eventually became fishers of men after their conversion. They were instrumental in spreading the gospel to the known world. For example, Stephen's martyr got the attention of a bystander named Saul who when converted, wrote two thirds of the New Testament becoming a great missionary and Apostle by divine providence (Acts, Chapters 8 and 9.)

FOR SISTERS ONLY

Allow me break this down in today's vernacular— right where we live. First to my sisters about, "MY BABY'S DADDY"—someone asked me, "What is my baby's daddy?" I was unfamiliar with the term too. Most of the time the term refers to the (boy/man) whom you thought was God's gift convince you to defy all your morals, principles, *and go against parental rule, advice and what you knew to be right. This would include God's commandments and code of conduct to have sex without the benefit, and honor of marriage to each other. The love of his life you were and your Prince Charming for life until you uttered those two killer words: I'M PREGNANT!" Suddenly, Prince Charming turns into <u>KING COBRA</u> slowly slithering out of your life rejecting all responsibility. Nor is <u>KC</u> willing to help you face the next nine months let alone a lifetime! What's ironic is you'll most likely rely on and need assistance from the same folks you refused to listen to in the first place. Let me pause to drop a heavier wisdom nugget. If you're contemplating having sex: think first. Think what do I really know about this person? What is their family history? What health issues are in their bloodline? These things will matter later on especially if you become pregnant and have a child with potentially all kinds of unexpected issues. The human DNA recreates what it's made of. In the heat of the moment, you don't think about this stuff. That's why you should "think" before the act and keep sexual activity within the bounds and sanctity of marriage.*

Family history is what all health professions require prior to something going wrong. Will you ask the same questions? There could be insanity, schizophrenia, life-threatening disease, abuse, molestation, etc. THINK!!!

Now he's conveniently coined as: "My baby's daddy." Surely he was there at conception. Where is he now or where has he been all nine months? During morning sicknesses, doctor visits, sporadic body changes, and body swellings in abdomen, hands, legs, feet? During midnight cravings, moments of uncertainty, silent cries of shame, financial insecurity, and pain-intensive labor where? God forbid the child is born with some abnormality. Will he be there for 2, 4, and 6AM feedings, walking the floor providing comfort and aide? Will you have to take him to court for child support? If you do get support, it may be enough to meet all the expenses. Most likely than not, you will have to go or return to work. In case you haven't heard or experienced, childcare is not cheap! Have you considered who will get the baby up, dressed and ready to be dropped off to the provider? Don't become distressed with the reality check. It's not male bashing but a wake up call for my sisters. The Word of God has always and will always be right.

FOR BROTHERS ONLY

Brothers, I want you to think about how every time you behave in this manner, you are losing something too. By carelessly sowing your seed, you are throwing away your inheritance. Sooner or later, you will have to support what's genetically yours! Yes, whenever your DNA proves to be in connection with you, you are thereby responsible and he/she has full rights to be apart of your life. Do the right thing until you are more mature, responsible or ready to settle down. So that your family will not be deprived of all it can be because you chose to be a careless lad who did things his way.

FOR BROTHERS & SISTERS

Brothers and sisters alike—let's keep it real. We all are marketable for Kingdom building. Using today's lingo, we got game: God-given gifts and talents. We all are precious in God's sight, fearfully and wonderfully made and marvelous in the eyes of God (Psalms 139:14). Yes marvelous! God made us in His image (Genesis 1:26-27). He created us individually to multiply (through the bonds and covenant of marriage) and replenish the earth becoming His ultimate family. The marriage bed will always be undefiled (Hebrews13:4). Marriage and childbearing within His law was intended to prevent us from experiencing the same problems that resulted from being disobedient to His commandments. Today, one of the biggest generational curses we battle is the spirit of "whoredom"—breeding generation after generation of unwed mothers and fathers. Yes, the many arising issues explicitly described within the contents of this book.

FOR PARENTS ONLY

Parents, we cannot bring foreigners (strangers) into our family unit and expect our children to readily approve or accept our choice. Please choose with precaution. You should never, never become involved in a relationship with someone who just wants you and not your children. This is one reason why you should at all costs; abstain from sex before marriage because it will surely cloud your judgment. You will be more readily to tolerate and overlook obvious signs of trouble that could resurface in the future. You will ignore all the red flags because your flesh will overrule and dominate your judgment. Your children are your responsibility. They didn't request to come here. Remember, they were yours before your meeting this new prospect. God has given you charge and stewardship to raise them in a healthy, holy and happy environment. Avoid the mistake of raising them up and giving them the impression there will never be another parent in their lives. Don't wallow in your sorrow while waiting on a good spouse to come along either. Children, who aren't properly acclimated to a new stepparent, are affected. How? Your children may end up really resenting your new partner, especially if your child and partner are both male. Some mothers allow their young sons to be the "man of the house" and when another man threatens that position, you've got mega-trouble! Trouble that interrupts the lives of everyone involved especially the children. Ladies, we have and will continue to raise wonderful sons; but truthfully, only a man can teach a boy how to become a man. One recommendation, find good, trusted mentors for your children. It still takes a village to raise a child! Don't attempt to do it alone. That is another classic reason of why God's way is always best. He already knew what His creation needed to function properly.

FOR GOD'S PEOPLE

Let's treat each other with respect, dignity, and agape love. Let's stop this low-level living, which yields less than desirable results. Living together, outside the marriage covenant, do not benefit the institution of marriage, family and society at large.

Don't allow anyone to convince or influence you otherwise. It is not ok. You will end up used and abused because of what you allowed to occur in your life. Know your worth. God has much invested in you. If you're saved, don't make the power of "Cross" ineffective in your life. There are untold benefits and riches that are hidden in God through Christ. You must belong to Him for the unveiling and revelation of all He has in store for you. There are countless treasures in our earthen vessels. So, wherever you find yourself in life at this very moment; know you have not gone so far, done so wrong or messed up so badly that God cannot help, heal and give you eternal hope. All you need is a made-up mind and a repentant heart (ready for change) and the capacity and desire to believe on the Lord Jesus Christ. God did it for me and He is no respecter of persons. He is a Promise Keeper and there is nothing is too hard for Him. His love for YOU is greater than any sin imaginable. Get off of the barstool of "wasted seasons" and rise up to the pulpit of purpose.

PRAYER OF RESTORATION

Psalm 23 is an excellent prayer for mind, soul and body restoration. After surviving life's battles, one can become weary and worn. This Psalm is the perfect remedy. Prayed by field shepherds after working long, hard days and enduring lonely nights. Jesus is our Good Shepherd, watching over and guarding our souls. He cares for and guides us when we allow Him to.

"Restore" implies putting back, replacing, reviving and setting aright some one or thing that is out of place or order. Our God does have an order, which he put in place when He created mankind. God's creation became a living soul as He breathed the breath of life into Adam (Genesis 2:7). And like Adam, we divert our attention and turn our conscience (mind, will, and emotion) away from the plan and order of God for our lives (Jeremiah 29:11-13).

Finding ourselves (souls) in unregenerate conditions and leading us into a path of unrighteousness. A path to an open desert and that's where the wiles (schemes, strategies) of the devil are launched (Ephesians 6:11).

Becoming increasingly thirsty and dry, desperately needing our souls restored to Gods original state and plan. From my own personal and often painful experience, I recommend if you need of an amazing prayer that will bring your soul into harmony with the Shepherd (Lord and Savior, Jesus Christ).

This Psalm of Comfort promises that you will:

- *Not want for anything (go lacking)*
- *Rest in peace and safety (for a weary soul)*
- *Receive a refreshing restoration (back to God)*
- *Remove fear in darkness (comfort and direction)*
- *Gain victory over your enemies (with supply of plenty)*
- *Have God's promise of goodness, grace and mercy (safe and peaceful dwelling for a lifetime.)*

A SPECIAL PRAYER FOR YOU

Father, in the name of Jesus, restore the souls of your people. Those who have been beaten down by life, poor choices and every form of abuse; we ask that You touch their hearts with your love. Remove every trace of unworthiness, low self-esteem and insecurity. Let them know if they have been abused in any manner (spiritually, mentally, verbally, physically or sexually) at whatever age or time period in their lives, that they are not the blame. It's not their fault, but that of spiritual wickedness in high places (all sin comes from the lies and deception of Satan who is a demonic spirit and the father of lies).

Release guilt from their minds so the may receive forgiveness for themselves and others whoever they may be. Allow them to know that You love them for who they are. Father, if they do not know You in the pardoning of their sins, save them right now by having them to repeat this simple prayer.

Lord Jesus, come into my heart now. I ask for forgiveness of my sins. I believe You died for my sins and rose on the third day with all power. Thank you for your victory over sin and death. Thank you for my new found life in You.
In the Name of Jesus Christ, A-men.

Welcome to the Family of God!

ABOUT THE AUTHOR

Rebecca Jean White is the proud mother of seven children—five daughters and two sons. Twenty-five grandchildren, one of whom is deceased, and sixteen great-grandchildren, one of whom is also deceased. She comes from a large family that consisted of thirteen siblings. She boasts that God gave her" a family, a tribe, and now a nation." Her family has been her inspiration in writing her debut book, "From the Barstool to the Pulpit."

Born in Shreveport, Louisiana (Caddo Parrish), she migrated to Philadelphia in the late forties with her family and was educated in the Philadelphia Public School System. She relocated to New Jersey with her military parents (deceased) in the fabulous fifties.

She began work, later married, and raised a family while building a career in several professions including Banking, Law Enforcement, Nursing, and working with Special Needs Children. Her passion, outside of teaching God's Word, is cooking. Known for her "highly requested", southern-style dishes, her culinary skills were inherited from her mother, who taught her how to cook at an early age.

Almost twenty-five years ago, she attended a revival in her hometown of Camden, New Jersey where she accepted the Lord as her personal Savior. Also, was water baptized in the same night—an experience that changed her life forever! With a continual hunger and thirst for spiritual substance, she began to seek a deeper relationship with Christ. Her quest led to the Baptism of the Holy Spirit with the evidence of speaking in other tongues.

Evangelist White attended a school of ministry for three years, where she was ordained. Since that time, her service in the Kingdom has involved several ministries including Janitorial Assistant, Tape Ministry Worker, Hospitality Coordinator, Head Usher, Pastoral Nurse, Assistant Pastor, Assistant Women's Director, Adult, and Teen Sunday School Teacher, and Events Coordinator.

She presently serves on the Ministerial Staff and Helps Ministry at Word Alive Church International (www.TheWordIsAlive.com) located in Manassas, Virginia, under the leadership of Bishop Wesley T. Cherry, Sr. (Th. D.)

Printed in the United States
203159BV00003B/199-441/P